World's favorite K-food,
BIBIMBAP
세계인이 사랑하는 K-푸드 **비빔밥**

World's favorite K-food,
BIBIMBAP

Author | Jhun, Ji-Young

Photographer | Choi, Hae-Sung
Art Director | Chung, Kang-Il

LEESCOM Publishing
Publisher | Lee, Jean-Hee
Editor | Hong, Da-Ye   Kim, Min-Ju
Editing Designer | Han, Song-Yi
Marketing Manager | Jang, Ki-Bong   Lee, Jin-Mork   Choi, Hye-Su

Published by LEESCOM Publishing Group (www.leescom.com)
#7151, 22, Teheran-ro 87-gil, Gangnam-gu, Seoul, Korea
Phone 82-2-540-5192
          82-2-544-5194
Fax 82-504-479-4222
Pub.R.N. | 2-3348

World's favorite K-food, BIBIMBAP
Copyright @ 2024 by Jhun, Ji-Young and LEESCOM Publishing
All right reserved, including the right of in whole or in part in any form.

ISBN 979-11-5616-779-2 (13590)

First Edition | September 2010
Second Edition | June 2024

Printed in Republic of Korea

Reviews from all over the world
전 세계인들이 극찬하는 비빔밥

Korean traditional dish Bibimbap was the most searched recipe on Google.
한국의 전통음식 비빔밥이 구글에서 가장 많이 검색된 레시피 1위에 올랐다.

- Google, 2023

We got seven different tastes, colors and personalities. There's a Korean food called Bibimbap, which it has several different materials and when you mix them, It becomes a great food. We're great group like that.
우리 일곱 명은 서로 다른 취향과 색깔, 성격을 지니고 있습니다. 한국에 비빔밥이라는 음식이 있어요. 여러 가지 재료가 들어가는데, 섞이면 훌륭한 음식이 되죠. 우리도 그런 그룹 같습니다.

- RM (BTS)

I make sure to eat only Korean food while I'm there. I particularly enjoy Bibimbap and Kimchi among other things. I eat kimchi quite often and I have been telling people that kimchi is the key to my figure.
한국에 오면 한국 음식만 먹는다. 한국 음식 중에서도 비빔밥과 김치를 가장 좋아한다. 김치는 평소에도 자주 먹는데, 사람들에게 내 몸매의 비결이라고 이야기하기도 한다.

- Sophie Marceau (Actress)

Bibimbap is the most well-liked Korean dish to everyone's liking. Perfection nutrition in one bowl, it will promote health and wellness for people around the world.
한식 중에서 세계인들의 입맛에 가장 잘 맞는 음식이 비빔밥입니다. 한 그릇에 완벽한 영양이 담긴 비빔밥은 한식을 대표하는 음식으로 세계인들의 건강을 책임질 것입니다.

- Seo, Kyoung-Duk (Professor · Korea PR Expert)

프롤로그

한국 음식문화를 대표하는 '비빔밥'

2023년 전 세계인들이 구글에서 가장 많이 검색한 요리법은 한식 '비빔밥'이었다고 합니다. 총 12개 항목 중 레시피 부문에서 한국의 비빔밥이 1위를 차지해 한식에 대한 세계적인 관심을 증명하고 있습니다.

기네스 펠트로와 팝의 황제 고 마이클 잭슨을 비롯한 유명 할리우드 스타들이 비빔밥 마니아라는 것은 잘 알려진 사실입니다.

한국의 대표 음식인 비빔밥은 한 그릇 안에 다양한 식재료가 어우러져 영양이 풍부한 웰빙음식이며 자연을 담은 아름다운 수채화 같은 음식입니다.

흰색의 쌀밥과 초록색의 시금치나물, 노란색의 계란, 빨간색의 당근과 검은색의 김가루나 표고버섯 등 한국의 상징인 오방색의 재료를 사용해서 시각적으로도 아름다운 조화를 이루고 있습니다.

한국 대표 음식인 비빔밥을 제대로 소개하는 책자가 없다는 것을 안타까워하던 차에 2010년 미국으로 출국하기 전, 서경덕 교수님의 도움으로 영어, 중국어, 스페인어, 일본어 4개국어로 번역하여 한국문화 홍보를 위해 사용하게 되었습니다. 14년이 지난 2024년 한국의 비빔밥이 전 세계적인 관심사가 되면서 영문으로 번역되어 다시 출간된다는 반가운 소식을 접하게 되었습니다.

    이제 비빔밥은 전 세계인이 궁금해하고 먹어보고 싶은 한국을 대표하는 음식이기도 한 동시에 한국인의 열정과 어우러짐을 상징하는 하나의 문화 아이콘이기도 합니다.
    비빔밥 책을 쓴 것이 계기가 되어 세계한인축제나 한국문화홍보 행사에서 대형 비빔밥 퍼포먼스 행사를 기획하기도 했습니다.

    이 책은 대중적으로 인기 있는 비빔밥, 퓨전 비빔밥, 다이어트 비빔밥과 지역별 전통 비빔밥에 대해 소개하고 있습니다. 이 중에서 지역별 전통 비빔밥은 각 지역의 전통적인 조리법을 중심으로 소개하였으나 재료나 식기 면에서 현대화된 부분이 있고 저자의 의견이 반영된 부분도 있습니다.

    출판에 도움을 주시고 해외에 비빔밥을 소개할 기회를 주신 리스컴 출판사 대표님과 관계자 분들께 감사드리며 그릇과 소품을 협찬해 주신 한국도자기, 한샘주방 대표님과 음식사진 촬영에 도움을 주신 김영숙, 홍종숙 님께도 깊은 감사의 마음을 전합니다. 아트디렉터로서 조언을 아끼지 않은 평생의 반려자 정강일 님께도 깊은 감사를 드립니다.

Jiyoung. J

Prologue

Representing Korean cuisine, Bibimbap

In 2023, the most searched recipe on Google worldwide was the Korean dish 'Bibimbap'. Among a total of 12 items, Korean bibimbap ranked first in the recipe category, proving the global interest in Korean food.

It is well known that famous Hollywood stars, including Gwyneth Paltrow and Pop Emperor Michael Jackson, were Bibimbap manias.

As a representative dish of Korea, Bibimbap is not only a low-calorie nutritious well-being food with various ingredients in a bowl, but also a beautiful watercolor with nature.

It is visually beautifully harmonized by using ingredients of the five colors, which are the symbols of Korea, such as white rice and green spinach, yellow eggs, red carrots and black seaweed flakes and shiitake mushrooms.
before leaving for the United States in 2010, with the help of Professor Seo Kyung-Duk, books in English, Chinese, Spanish, and Japanese were published, and these were used to promote Korean culture.

Fourteen years later, in 2024, Korean bibimbap became a global concern, and I received good news that it will be translated into English and published again.

Now, Bibimbap is a representative Korean cuisine that people all over the world want to know and try, at the same time, it is a cultural icon that symbolizes harmony with the passion of Korean.

Because of the publication of the Bibimbap book, I had the opportunity to organize large-scale bibimbap performance events at Korean festivals and Korean culture promotion events around the world.

The book introduces Popular Bibimbap, Fusion Bibimbap, Diet Bibimbap, and local Traditional Bibimbap. Among them, Traditional Bibimbap was introduced centering on the traditional recipes of each region, but there were some modernized parts in terms of ingredients and tableware, and some parts reflected the author's opinion.

I would like to thank the CEO of LEEESCOM Publishing and officials for helping to publish and introducing Bibimbap abroad, and I would like to express my deep gratitude to Korean ceramics and Hanssem Kitchen for sponsoring bowls and props, as well as Kim Young-Sook and Hong Jong-Sook for helping to take food photos. Finally, I would like to deeply thank my lifelong partner, Chung Kang-Il, for his advice as an art director.

Contents

- 3 전 세계가 극찬하는 비빔밥
  Review from all over the world
- 4 프롤로그
- 6 Prologue
- 10 완벽한 한 그릇, 비빔밥
- 12 Perfection in a bowl, Bibimbap
- 14 비빔밥의 기본
- 16 The basic of Bibimbap

Chapter 1

Popular Bibimbap 인기 비빔밥

- 28 불고기 비빔밥
- 30 Bulgogi Bibimbap
- 32 돌솥 비빔밥
- 34 Dolsot Bibimbap
- 36 돼지고기김치볶음 비빔밥
- 38 Fried Pork and Kimchi Bibimbap
- 40 낙지 비빔밥
- 42 Octopus Bibimbap
- 44 부추 비빔밥
- 46 Chive Bibimbap
- 48 꼬막 비빔밥
- 50 Cockle Bibimbap
- 52 회생채 비빔밥
- 54 Bibimbap with Sashimi
- 56 굴무밥
- 58 Oyster rice with Soy sauce
- 60 양송이버섯 비빔밥
- 62 Mushroom Bibimbap
- 64 우렁강된장 비빔밥
- 66 Soybean paste Bibimbap

Chapter 2

Fusion Bibimbap 퓨전 비빔밥

- 70   참치마요네즈 비빔밥
- 72   Tuna Mayonnaise Bibimbap
- 74   비빔밥 피자
- 76   Bibimbap Pizza
- 78   비빔밥 크레이프
- 80   Bibimbap Crepes
- 82   떡갈비 비빔밥
- 84   Bibimbap Tteokgalbi
- 86   유부 비빔밥
- 88   Fried Tofu Bibimbap
- 90   찹쌀고기말이 비빔밥
- 92   Bibimbap Beef Roll
- 94   비빔밥 옥수수전
- 96   Bibimbap Pancake
- 98   비빔밥 크로켓
- 100 Bibimbap Croquette
- 102 잡곡 비빔밥 케이크
- 104 Multigrain Bibimbap Cake
- 106 비빔 꼬마 김밥
- 108 Little Gimbap with Bibimbap

Chapter 3

Bibimbap for dieting 다이어트 비빔밥

- 112 산채 비빔밥
- 114 Sanchae Bibimbap
- 116 채소샐러드 비빔밥
- 118 Vegetable salad Bibimbap
- 120 단호박 비빔밥
- 122 Pumpkin Bibimbap
- 124 콩나물 비빔밥
- 126 Bean sprouts Bibimbap
- 128 두부 간장 비빔밥
- 130 Tofu Bibimbap with Soy sauce
- 132 도토리묵 비빔밥
- 134 Acorn jello Bibimbap
- 136 비빔 쌈밥
- 138 Bibimbap with Vegetable wraps
- 140 무생채 비빔밥
- 142 Spicy Radish Salad Bibimbap

Chapter 4

Traditional Bibimbap 전통 비빔밥

- 146 전주 비빔밥
- 148 Jeonju-style Bibimbap
- 150 평양 비빔밥
- 152 Pyongyang-style Bibimbap
- 154 안동 비빔밥
- 156 Andong-style Bibimbap
- 158 통영 비빔밥
- 160 Tongyoung-style Bibimbap
- 162 평안도 비빔밥
- 164 Pyongahndo-style Bibimbap
- 166 Glossary of Korean Cooking

완벽한 한 그릇, 비빔밥

한국의 대표 음식인 비빔밥이 이제는 세계인의 입맛을 사로잡았다. 비빔밥은 저칼로리 다이어트식이면서 여러 가지 식품이 고루 들어가 5대 영양소의 균형도 잘 맞는 완벽한 음식이다.

세계인의 건강식으로 안성맞춤!

비빔밥은 밥에 고기와 여러 가지 나물을 넣고 비벼 먹는 음식이다. 다양한 재료가 고루 들어가 영양의 균형이 잘 잡혀 있다. 비빔밥의 주재료는 쌀인데, 쌀은 빵이나 국수보다는 혈당지수가 낮다. 혈당지수가 낮은 음식은 당뇨병을 비롯한 성인병을 예방하는 효과가 있다. 쌀은 혈압 상승을 억제하는 작용도 한다.
비빔밥을 구성하는 또 다른 재료인 채소는 비타민 C나 엽산 등이 풍부해 노화를 억제시키는 효과가 있다. 채소에 함유된 섬유질은 변비를 예방해주고, 몸에 해로운 중금속이 우리 몸 안에 흡수되는 것을 막아준다.

쌀을 주재료로 한 웰빙 음식

쌀은 다른 곡물보다 소화·흡수가 잘 된다. 쌀의 주성분은 탄수화물 79%, 단백질은 7% 정도로 구성되어 있다. 단백질 중에서도 필수아미노산의 일종인 리신의 함량이 높아서 콜레스테롤 수치를 떨어뜨리는 효과가 있다. 이밖에도 쌀에는 칼슘, 철분, 인, 칼륨, 나트륨, 마그네슘 같은 미네랄이 고루 들어 있다.

영양 균형이 완벽한 한 그릇

아무리 우수한 식품이라도 한 가지만 오래 먹으면 영양 불균형이 되기 쉽다. 하지만 비빔밥은 우리 몸이 필요로 하는 탄수화물, 단백질, 지방 등 여러 가지 영양소를 골고루 갖고 있다. 그래서 비빔밥 한 그릇이면 대부분의 영양을 충족시킬 수 있다.

저칼로리 다이어트 음식

비빔밥은 다이어트에 효과적이다. 밥은 빵이나 국수보다 칼로리가 적고, 음식이 소화·흡수되는 데 걸리는 시간도 길기 때문에 포만감이 오래 간다. 비빔밥 소스로 이용되는 고추장도 다이어트에 효과가 있다. 고추장의 캡사이신 성분이 몸에서 땀이 나도록 해서 노폐물 배설을 촉진시킨다.

자연과 환경을 생각한 요리

제철에 나는 신선한 채소를 다양하게 활용하는 요리가 비빔밥이다. 또 육식을 많이 할수록 목축업으로 인한 환경오염이 심해지는데, 육류보다 채소의 비중이 높은 비빔밥은 대표적인 환경 친화 식품이다.

전통 발효식품을 활용한 건강한 음식

비빔밥 소스로 사용되는 고추장이나 된장, 간장 등 한국의 전통 발효식품은 발효 과정에서 여러 가지 생리 활성물질이 늘어나 몸에 좋은 작용을 한다. 이들 발효식품은 항암 효과가 뛰어나며 혈압을 낮추는 데도 좋다. 몸의 해독작용을 도와주기도 한다.

Perfection in a bowl, Bibimbap

Korean representative dish, Bibimbap is enticing the taste buds of people at every corner of the world. Bibimbap is perfect for a low-calorie diet and with five essential nutrients in its ingredients, the dish is nutritionally balanced.

Ideal for a healthy diet

Bibimbap is a dish to be stirred together with rice, meat and seasoned vegetables, which makes it balanced nutritionally. Its main ingredient, rice, contains lower blood glucose than bread or noodles. Food low in blood glucose is effective in preventing lifestyle diseases such as diabetes.
Rice also acts to suppress the increase in blood pressure. Vegetables in bibimbap contain vitamin C and folic acid, effective in slowing down aging while vegetables high in fiber provides a relief from constipation and prevents the absorption of contaminants in the body.

A well-being dish featuring rice

Rice is much easily digested than other grains. It is mainly composed of 79% carbohydrates and 7% protein. Especially high in lysine, one of essential amino acids, rice helps to lower the cholesterol level. On top of it, it is rich in minerals like calcium, iron, phosphorus, potassium, sodium and magnesium.

High-nutrition all-in-one meal

No matter how rich in nutrients, a long-term consumption of one type of nutrient could lead to an imbalance. In this respect, bibimbap has an assortment of carbohydrate, protein and fat all in one. With a bowl of bibimbap, you can satisfy the daily nutrient requirement.

Low-calorie diet food

Bibimbap is highly effective in dieting. Calorie in a bowl of rice is lower than that of bread or noodles. The time it takes for absorption in the body is longer than its counterparts, prolonging the satiated feeling longer. Red pepper paste for bibimbap seasoning also helps dieting in that capsaicin in the paste stimulates sweating and promote the excretion of body wastes.

Food that cares about nature and environment

Bibimbap is known to use fresh, seasonal vegetables in various ways. With more meat consumption, the pollution created by livestock production is reaching a critical level. Bibimbap, with its main ingredients being vegetables, is also eco-friendly.

Healthy dish with fermented ingredients

Korean seasonings such as red pepper paste, soybean paste and soy sauce, acquire active substances during the fermentation, which benefits the body. These fermented ingredients have anti carcinogenic properties and works to lower the blood pressure. They also aid in detoxification.

비빔밥의 기본

맛있는 밥 짓기

비빔밥을 맛있게 만들기 위해서는 밥짓기를 잘해야 한다. 맛있는 밥을 지으려면 좋은 쌀을 고르고, 물에 잘 씻고, 물 양을 알맞게 맞추고, 불의 세기를 잘 조절하고, 뜸을 잘 들여야 한다. 압력밥솥을 이용하면 밥짓기가 한결 쉽다.

좋은 쌀 선택하기

쌀 알갱이가 통통하고 윤기가 나며 쌀알의 표면이 부서지지 않은 것이 좋다. 도정한 지 15일 이내의 쌀에 수분 함량이 많기 때문에 바로 도정한 쌀일수록 밥을 지으면 맛있게 된다.

쌀 씻기

가장 먼저, 쌀에 물을 가득 부은 뒤 손으로 대충 휘저어서 빨리 헹군다. 그 다음, 물을 적게 붓고 손으로 문질러 씻은 다음 물에 헹군다. 이 과정을 3~4번 반복한다.

Tip 쌀을 씻을 때는 쌀눈이 떨어져 나가지 않도록 살살 씻는 것이 좋다.

쌀 불리기

쌀을 씻고 나서 30분 정도 물에 담가 둔다. 압력밥솥일 때는 불리는 과정을 생략해도 된다.

밥 짓기

불린 상태의 쌀 분량의 1.2배가량의 물이 적당하다. 도정한 지 오래 된 쌀은 이보다 물을 조금 더 넣고, 갓 수확한 쌀은 수분이 많으므로 물을 조금 적게 넣는다.

불 조절하기

처음에 센 불에서 익히고 밥물이 끓으면 약한 불로 줄인다. 어느 정도 익었을 때 냄비의 뚜껑을 열어봐야 하는데, 이때 밥 위에 물기가 스며들었다면 아주 약한 불로 줄여서 10분 정도 더 익혀 뜸을 들인다. 뜸을 들인 후에는 뚜껑을 열고 주걱으로 밥을 뒤섞어 수분을 날려준다. 그렇지 않으면 뚜껑 위에 맺힌 물방울이 밥 위로 떨어져 밥맛을 떨어뜨린다.

잡곡밥 짓기

잡곡은 종류마다 익는 속도가 다르기 때문에 물에 불리거나 삶는 시간이 모두 다르다. 딱딱한 콩은 반나절 정도 물에 불리고 수수, 좁쌀은 쌀과 함께 30분가량만 불린다. 팥은 미리 삶아서 쓴다. 물은 쌀로만 지을 때보다 대략 1/10 정도 더 넣는 것이 좋다.

현미밥 짓기

물은 쌀로만 지을 때보다 조금 넉넉히 붓는다. 일반 밥솥에 지을 때는 현미의 1.5배, 압력밥솥을 이용할 때는 1.2배의 물을 붓고 1시간 이상 담가 두었다가 밥을 짓는다.

The basic of Bibimbap

Cooking rice

In order to make a delicious bibimbap, we need to cook the rice properly. Well-cooked rice needs good quality rice rinsed properly, the right amount of water, the water pressure and good steaming.

Choosing the good rice

A full and polished rice is necessary and the surface should not be broken. The sooner the polishing, the nicer the cooked rice because the rice contains a lot of moisture within 15 days after polishing.

Washing the rice

First, fill the washing container with water then stir quickly using the hand. Next, pour just a little amount of water to lightly scrub the grain to get rid of the hulls and stir the water. Repeat 3 to 4 times.

> **Tip** When you wash the rice, you must be careful not to scrub off the embryo bud of each grain.

Soaking the rice

After washing the rice, soak it for 30 min. If you are using a pressure rice maker, you can skip this step.

Making rice

The right amount of water is about 1.2 times the amount of soaked rice. If the rice has long been polished, pour a little more water and the other way around with just polished rice.

Adjusting the fire

The fire should be strong at first and weakened as the water starts boiling. The lid should be opened to check the process. If the water has been absorbed, weaken the fire and leave it for another 10 min. This step is called "steaming".
After steaming, be quick to release the lid and mix the cooked rice thoroughly to blow off the leftover moisture. If you skip this step, the water bubbles on the lid drop on the rice and make it less tasteful.

Making multigrain rice

Every grain has a different period of time to get fully cooked.
Hard beans should be soaked for half a day while African millet and Hulled millet for 30 min like white rice. Red-bean should be boiled beforehand. Then, pour around 1/10 more water than with just white rice.

Making brown rice

It requires more water than white rice. You need 1.5 times as much water as the amount of brown rice when using a rice maker and 1.2 times as much for a pressure rice maker. Soak it for at least an hour before cooking the rice.

비빔밥의 기본

맛있는 나물 만들기

생채소부터 익힌 채소, 산채까지 비빔밥에 들어가는 채소의 종류는 매우 다양하다.
비빔밥의 필수 재료인 나물을 만들어보자.

숙채 나물

• 콩나물

재료_ 콩나물 200g, 소금 조금, 물 2큰술
양념_ 소금(또는 국간장) ½큰술, 다진 파·다진 마늘 1작은술씩, 깨소금·참기름 ½큰술씩
만드는 법_ ① 콩나물을 다듬어 씻는다. ② 냄비에 콩나물을 안친 후 물과 소금을 조금 넣고 뚜껑을 덮어 삶는다. ③ 건져서 식힌 후 양념을 모두 넣고 무친다.

• 숙주나물

재료_ 숙주 200g, 소금 조금, 물 적당량
양념_ 소금(또는 국간장) ½큰술, 다진 파·다진 마늘 1작은술씩, 깨소금·참기름 ½큰술씩
만드는 법_ ① 숙주를 깨끗이 씻는다. ② 끓는 물에 소금을 조금 넣고 숙주를 잠깐 데친다. ③ 건져서 식힌 후 양념을 모두 넣고 무친다.

• 시금치나물

재료_ 시금치 200g, 소금 조금
양념_ 소금(또는 국간장) ½큰술, 다진 파·다진 마늘 1작은술씩, 깨소금·참기름 ½큰술씩
만드는 법_ ① 끓는 물에 소금을 조금 넣고 시금치를 데쳐서 찬물에 헹군다. ② 물기를 꼭 짠 후 양념을 모두 넣고 무친다.

• 미나리나물

재료_ 미나리 200g, 소금 조금
양념_ 소금(또는 국간장) ½큰술, 다진 파·다진 마늘 1작은술씩, 깨소금·참기름 ½큰술씩
만드는 법_ ① 미나리는 잎을 잘라내고 줄기만 다듬어 깨끗이 씻은 후 끓는 물에 소금을 조금 넣고 데친다. ② 찬물에 헹구어 물기를 짜고 5cm 길이로 썬다. ③ 양념을 모두 넣고 무친다.

• **배추무침나물**

재료_ 얼갈이배추 200g, 소금 조금

양념_ 소금 ½큰술, 다진 파·다진 마늘 1작은술씩, 깨소금·참기름 ½큰술씩

만드는 법_ ① 끓는 물에 소금을 조금 넣고 얼갈이배추를 데쳐서 찬물에 헹군다. ② 물기를 짜고 먹기 좋게 썬다. ③ 양념을 모두 넣고 무친다.

Tip 소금 대신 된장으로 무치기도 한다.

• **가지나물**

재료_ 가지 1개

양념_ 간장 2작은술, 다진 파 ½큰술, 다진 마늘 1작은술, 참기름 2작은술, 깨소금 1작은술

만드는 법_ ① 가지는 반 갈라 찜통에 넣고 찐다. ② 살짝 쪄지면 꺼내서 식혀 굵게 찢는다. ③ 양념을 모두 넣고 무친다.

• **냉이나물**

재료_ 냉이 200g

양념_ 된장 1큰술, 다진 파 ½큰술, 깨소금·참기름 ½큰술씩, 다진 마늘 ½작은술

만드는 법_ ① 냉이는 다듬어 씻은 후 끓는 물에 데쳐서 찬물에 헹군다. ② 물기를 꼭 짠 후 양념을 넣고 무친다.

Tip 된장 대신 고추장으로 무쳐도 좋다.

생채 나물

• **무생채**

재료_ 무 200g, 소금 ½큰술

양념_ 고춧가루 ½큰술, 설탕·식초 1큰술씩, 다진 파 1큰술, 다진 마늘 ½작은술, 깨소금 2작은술, 소금 조금

만드는 법_ ① 무는 껍질을 벗기고 채 썬 다음 소금을 조금 뿌려 절이고 물기를 꼭 짠다. ② 절인 무채에 고춧가루를 넣고 버무린다. ③ 나머지 양념을 모두 넣고 무친다.

• **부추무침**

재료_ 부추 200g, 소금 ½큰술

양념_ 간장 ½큰술, 멸치액젓 2작은술고, 고춧가루 ½큰술, 다진 파·마늘 1큰술씩, 설탕·식초 ½큰술씩, 참기름 2작은술, 소금·깨소금 조금씩

만드는 법_ ① 부추를 깨끗이 씻어 물기를 뺀 뒤 5cm 길이로 자른다. ② 양념을 모두 넣고 버무린다.

볶음 나물

• 애호박나물

재료_ 애호박 1개, 소금 조금, 식용유 1큰술
양념_ 새우젓 1큰술, 다진 파 1큰술, 다진 마늘 1/2큰술, 깨소금·참기름·소금 조금씩

만드는 법_ ① 애호박을 반달 모양으로 썬 뒤 소금에 살짝 절였다가 물기를 짠다. ② 기름 두른 팬에 애호박을 볶다가 새우젓, 다진 파, 다진 마늘을 넣어 볶는다. ③ 참기름과 깨소금을 넣고 섞는다.

> **Tip** 애호박을 소금에 절이지 않고 볶으면 너무 물렁거리고 부서지기 쉽다.

• 무나물

재료_ 무 250g, 식용유 1큰술
양념_ 국간장 ½큰술, 다진 파 ½큰술, 다진 마늘 1작은술, 생강즙 ½작은술, 참기름 ½큰술, 깨소금 조금

만드는 법_ ① 무는 껍질을 벗기고 채 썬다. ② 팬에 기름을 두르고 무채를 볶는다. ③ 물을 붓고 익히다 양념을 모두 넣고 볶는다.

> **Tip** 무는 들기름으로 볶아도 좋다.

• 도라지나물

재료_ 도라지 100g, 소금 조금, 식용유 적당량
양념_ 국간장·다진 파 ½큰술씩, 다진 마늘·깨소금 1작은술씩, 참기름 ½큰술, 생강즙·소금 조금씩, 물 2큰술

만드는 법_ ① 도라지는 소금을 뿌려 주무른 뒤 찬물에 여러 번 헹구고 먹기 좋게 자른다. ② 끓는 물에 도라지를 데친 후 다시 한번 헹군다. ③ 팬에 기름을 두르고 국간장, 다진 파·마늘, 생강즙을 넣어 볶다가 물을 붓고 익힌다. 마지막에 깨소금, 참기름을 넣어 맛을 낸다.

• 고사리나물

재료_ 마른 고사리 70g, 식용유 1큰술, 물 ⅓컵
양념_ 국간장 1큰술, 다진 파 ½큰술, 다진 마늘 2작은술, 깨소금·참기름 ½큰술씩

만드는 법_ ① 마른 고사리는 물에 충분히 불려서 삶은 후 물에 여러 번 우려서 물기를 짠다. ② 5cm 길이로 썰어 양념에 무친 후 간이 배게 둔다. ③ 팬에 식용유를 두르고 양념한 고사리를 볶다가 물을 붓고 뚜껑을 덮어 약한 불로 익힌다.

• 취나물

재료_ 마른 취 70g, 식용유 1큰술, 물 ½컵
양념_ 국간장 1½큰술, 다진 파 ½큰술, 다진 마늘 2작은술, 깨소금·참기름 ½큰술씩

만드는 법_ ① 마른 취를 삶아서 물에 충분히 불린 뒤 물기를 가볍게 짠다. ② 삶은 취에 양념을 넣고 무친다. ③ 팬에 기름을 두르고 양념한 취나물을 볶는다. 중간중간 물을 넣어가며 부드럽게 익힌다.

• **깻잎나물**

재료_ 깻잎 200g, 식용유 1큰술, 물 1½큰술
양념_ 국간장 1큰술, 다진 파 ½큰술, 다진 마늘 2작은술, 깨소금·참기름 ½큰술씩

만드는 법_ ① 깻잎은 끓는 물에 소금을 조금 넣고 데쳐서 물기를 꼭 짠다. ② 깻잎에 양념을 넣어 무친다. ③ 팬에 식용유를 두르고 깻잎을 볶다가 물을 넣고 부드럽게 볶는다.

Tip 깻잎은 들기름으로 볶아도 좋다.

• **시래기나물**

재료_ 시래기 50g, 식용유 1큰술, 물 ⅓컵
양념_ 된장 2작은술, 국간장 2작은술, 다진 파·다진 마늘 ½큰술씩, 깨소금·참기름 1큰술씩

만드는 법_ ① 말린 시래기는 물에 충분히 담가 불린 뒤 여러 번 헹군다. ② 불린 시래기의 물기를 꼭 짠 뒤 적당한 길이로 잘라 양념으로 무친다. ③ 팬에 기름을 두르고 양념한 시래기를 볶다가 물을 붓고 부드럽게 익힌다.

그 밖의 볶음 나물

• **표고버섯볶음**

재료_ 표고버섯 100g, 식용유 ½큰술
양념_ 소금 1작은술, 다진 마늘 1작은술, 참기름·깨소금 1작은술씩

만드는 법_ ① 생 표고버섯은 물에 씻은 뒤 기둥을 잘라내고 굵게 채 썬다. ② 기름 두른 팬에 표고버섯을 넣고 양념을 모두 넣어 볶는다.

• **당근볶음**

재료_ 당근 100g, 소금 1작은술, 식용유 1큰술

만드는 법_ ① 당근을 손질해 채 썬다. ② 팬에 기름을 두르고 당근을 볶는다. 중간에 소금으로 간한다.

The basic of Bibimbap

Preparing the Various Vegetables

From fresh vegetables, cooked vegetables to herbs, Bibimbap's ingredients are diverse. Let's try making bibimbap's must-have ingredient, Namul. If you know the basics, you can apply it to any other kind of vegetables.

Boiled Namul

• Bean sprouts

Ingredients_ 200g of bean sprouts, a little salt, 2Ts water

Seasoning_ ½Ts salt(or soy sauce), 1ts chopped leek, 1ts crushed garlic, ½Ts ground sesame, ½Ts sesame oil

Preparation_ ① Clean and wash bean sprouts. ② Put prepared bean sprouts, water and salt in a pot, then cover and parboil them. ③ Take out and let them cool, then throw in the seasoning and massage it.

• Green bean sprouts

Ingredients_ 200g of green bean sprouts, a little salt, enough water

Seasoning_ ½Ts salt(or soy sauce), 1ts chopped leek, 1ts crushed garlic, ½Ts ground sesame, ½Ts sesame oil

Preparation_ ① Wash green bean sprouts. ② Parboil prepared green bean sprouts in boiling water with a little salt. ③ Take out and let them cool, then throw in the seasoning and massage it.

• Spinach

Ingredients_ 200g of spinach, a little salt

Seasoning_ ½Ts salt(or soy sauce), 1ts chopped leek, 1ts crushed garlic, ½Ts ground sesame, ½Ts sesame oil

Preparation_ ① Parboil the spinach in boiling water with a little salt and rinse them under cold water. ② Squeeze out water, then throw in the seasoning and massage it.

• Water parsley

Ingredients_ 200g of water parsley, a little salt

Seasoning_ ½Ts salt(or soy sauce), 1ts chopped leek, 1ts crushed garlic, ½Ts ground sesame, ½Ts sesame oil

Preparation_ ① Take off leaves and wash the water parsley, then parboil them in boiling water with a little salt. ② Rinse boiled water parsley under cold water and squeeze out, then cut them in 5cm. ③ Throw in the seasoning and massage it.

- **Kimchi cabbage**

Ingredients_ 200g of kimchi cabbage, a little salt
Seasoning_ ½Ts salt, 1ts chopped leek, 1ts crushed garlic, ½Ts ground sesame, ½Ts sesame oil

Preparation_ ① Parboil the kimchi cabbage in boiling water with a little salt and rinse them under cold water. ② Squeeze out water and cut them bite-size. ③ Throw in the seasoning and massage it.

> **Tip** It is good to use soybean paste instead of salt.

- **Eggplant**

Ingredients_ 1 eggplant
Seasoning_ 2ts soy sauce, ½Ts chopped leek, 1ts crushed garlic, 2ts sesame oil, 1ts ground sesame

Preparation_ ① Cut the eggplant in half and steam it in the steamer. ② When the eggplant slightly cooked, take out and let it cool. After, tear cooked eggplant thickly. ③ Throw in the seasoning and massage it.

- **Shepherd's purse**

Ingredients_ 200g of shepherd's purse
Seasoning_ 1Ts soybean paste, ½Ts chopped leek, ½Ts ground sesame, ½Ts sesame oil, ½ts crushed garlic

Preparation_ ① Parboil the shepherd's purse in boiling water after cleaning and washing them, then rinse boiled shepherd's purse under cool water. ② After squeeze out water, throw in the seasoning and massage it.

> **Tip** It is good to use red pepper paste instead of soybean paste.

Salad Namul

- **Spicy Radish Salad**

Ingredients_ 200g of radish, ½Ts salt
Seasoning_ ½Ts red pepper powder, 1Ts sugar, 1Ts vinegar, 1Ts chopped leek, ½ts crushed garlic, 2ts ground sesame and a little salt

Preparation_ ① Peel and shred the radish, then squeeze out water after salt them. ② Mix salted radish with red pepper powder. ③ Throw in the rest of seasoning and massage it.

• Chive Salad

Ingredients_ 200g of chive, ½Ts salt
Seasoning_ ½Ts soy sauce, 2ts salted anchovy sauce, ½Ts red pepper powder, 1Ts chopped leek, 1Ts crushed garlic, ½Ts sugar, ½Ts vinegar, 2ts sesame oil, a little salt and ground sesame

Preparation_ ① Wash chives and squeeze out water, then cut them in 5cm. ② Throw in the seasoning and massage it.

Stir-fried Namul

• Zucchini

Ingredients_ 1 zucchini, a little salt, 1Ts cooking oil
Seasoning_ 1Ts salted shrimp, 1Ts chopped leek, ½Ts crushed garlic, a little bit each of ground sesame, sesame oil and salt

Preparation_ ① Cut the zucchini into half-moon shape and salt them, then squeeze out water. ② Sauté the zucchini in the frying pan with oil first, then sauté more with salted shrimp, chopped leek, and crushed garlic. Put sesame oil and ground sesame.

 Tip If you don't salt the zucchini before cooking, it is easy to become squashy.

• Bellflower root

Ingredients_ 100g of bellflower root, a little salt, enough cooking oil
Seasoning_ ½Ts soy sauce, ½Ts chopped leek, 1ts crushed garlic, 1ts ground sesame, ½Ts sesame oil, a little salt and ginger juice, 2Ts water

Preparation_ ① After mix the bellflower root and salt, rinse them under cool water several times and cut bite-size. ② Parboil the bellflower root in boiling water and rinse again. ③ Sauté boiled bellflower root with soy sauce, chopped leek, crushed garlic and ginger juice in the frying pan with oil, then add some water and cook more. Lastly, Put ground sesame and sesame oil.

• Bracken

Ingredients_ 70g of dried bracken, 1Ts cooking oil, ⅓cup of water
Seasoning 1Ts soy sauce, ½Ts chopped leek, 2ts crushed garlic, ½Ts sesame oil, ½Ts ground sesame

Preparation_ ① After soak dried bracken in water for a while, boil them and squeeze out water. ② Cut boiled bracken in 5cm and season. ③ Sauté seasoned bracken in the frying pan with cooking oil, then cover and cook over a low heat.

• Aster

Ingredients_ 70g of dried aster, 1Ts cooking oil, ⅓cup of water
Seasoning_ 1½Ts soy sauce, ½Ts chopped leek, 2ts crushed garlic, ½Ts ground sesame, ½Ts sesame oil

Preparation_ ① After soak dried aster in water for a while, boil them and squeeze out water. ② Mix boiled aster and the seasoning. ③ Sauté seasoned aster in the frying pan with oil. Cook well adding some water.

• Sesame leaves

Ingredients_ 200g of sesame leaves, 1Ts cooking oil, 1½Ts water
Seasoning_ 1Ts soy sauce, ½Ts chopped leek, 2ts crushed garlic, ½Ts ground sesame, ½Ts sesame oil

Preparation_ ① Parboil the sesame leaves in boiling water with a little salt, then squeeze out water. ② Season boiled sesame leaves with seasonings. ③ Sauté seasoned sesame leaves in the frying pan with cooking oil, then add some water and cook more.

> **Tip** It is good to use soybean paste instead of salt.

• Dried radish leaves

Ingredients_ 50g of dried radish leaves, 1Ts cooking oil, ⅓cup of water
Seasoning_ 2ts soybean paste, 2ts soy sauce, ½Ts chopped leek, ½Ts crushed garlic, 1Ts ground sesame, 1Ts sesame oil

Preparation_ ① Soak dried radish leaves in water for a while, then rinse them under water several times.
② After squeeze out water, cut the radish leaves in bite-size and season.
③ Sauté seasoned radish leaves in the frying pan with oil, then add some water and cook more.

Other stir-fried vegetables

• Stir-fried Shiitake

Ingredients_ 100g of shiitake, ½Ts cooking oil
Seasoning_ 1ts salt, 1ts crushed garlic, 1ts ground sesame, 1ts sesame oil

Preparation_ ① After wash the shiitake, take off roots and shred thickly.
② Sauté the shiitake and the seasoning in the frying pan with oil.

• Stir-fried Carrot

Ingredients_ 100g of carrot, 1ts salt, 1Ts cooking oil

Preparation_ ① Prepare and shred the carrot. ② Sauté them in the frying pan with oil, then add a little salt.

Chapter

Popular Bibimbap 인기 비빔밥

Bibimbap has changed over the years. In this chapter are popular Bibimbap dishes including Bibimbap cooked in sizzling hot stone pots, Bulgogi Bibimbap, Chive Bibimbap, and Bibimbap with Sashimi.

비빔밥도 시대에 따라 여러 가지로 변화되었다. 뜨거운 돌솥에 지글지글 익으며 나오는 돌솥 비빔밥을 비롯해서 불고기 비빔밥, 부추 비빔밥, 회생채 비빔밥까지 인기 비빔밥을 모두 모았다.

불고기 비빔밥

우리나라 대표 요리인 불고기로 만든 비빔밥. 모양 내서 담아 손님상에 내기에 좋다.

재료 (2인분)

현미밥 2공기
채소샐러드 적당량

불고기

쇠고기 100g
다진 파·마늘 2작은술씩
간장·배즙 1큰술씩
설탕 ½큰술
깨소금·참기름 조금씩
식용유 1큰술

나물 (40g씩)

깻잎나물
당근볶음

양념고추장

고추장 3큰술
물엿 1큰술
매실액 ½큰술
다진 마늘 2작은술
참기름 2작은술

만드는 법

1. 쇠고기는 다진 파, 다진 마늘, 간장, 배즙, 설탕, 깨소금, 참기름으로 양념해 기름 두른 팬에 볶는다.
2. 깻잎나물을 만들어 준비해둔다. (p.21 참조)
3. 당근을 볶아서 준비한다. (p.21 참조)
4. 현미밥을 준비해 원형 틀에 꾹꾹 눌러 담아 납작한 모양을 만든다. 2인분 6개를 만든다.
5. 둥근 현미밥 위에 양념고추장을 바르고 깻잎나물, 현미밥, 당근볶음, 현미밥 순으로 올린다. 맨 위에 양념고추장을 바르고 불고기를 얹는다.
6. 채소샐러드를 준비해 접시에 비빔밥과 함께 담는다.

Bulgogi Bibimbap

Bibimbap dish with Bulgogi, a well-known Korean beef dish. It's pretty with layers of different colors.

Ingredients (2 servings)

2 bowls of cooked brown rice
Some of vegetable salad

Bulgogi
100g of beef
2ts crushed garlic
2ts chopped leek
1Ts soy sauce
1Ts pear juice
½Ts sugar
a little bit of sesame oil and ground sesame
1Ts cooking oil

Seasoned vegetable (40g)
Sesame leaves
Stir-fried carrot

Seasoned red pepper paste
3Ts red pepper paste
1Ts starch syrup
½Ts plum extract
2ts crushed garlic
2ts sesame oil

Preparation

1. Season prepared portion of beef with chopped leek, crushed garlic, soy sauce, and pear juice. Stir-fry on a pan.
2. Prepare seasoned sesame leaves. (see p.25)
3. Season the shredded carrots. (see p.25)
4. Prepare cooked brown rice and shape into round, flat portions. 3 portions make one serving.
5. Spread seasoned red pepper paste on rice portion and place easoned sesame leaves, rice, fried carrots, and rice in the order mentioned.
6. Serve on a plate with vegetable salad.

돌솥 비빔밥

각종 나물과 쇠고기 육회, 달걀노른자를 달군 돌솥에 올려 쓱쓱 비벼 먹는 비빔밥

재료 (2인분)

밥 2공기
고추기름 조금
상추 2장
김가루 2큰술
달걀노른자 2개

쇠고기 육회

쇠고기 50g
배즙·청주·간장·참기름·깨소금
다진 양파·다진 마늘·
후춧가루·잣가루 조금씩

각종 나물 (40g씩)

콩나물·시금치나물·애호박나물·
무나물·도라지나물·고사리나물·
취나물·표고버섯볶음·당근볶음

양념고추장

고추장 3큰술, 물엿 1큰술
매실액 2작은술
다진 마늘 2작은술
참기름 2작은술

만드는 법

1. 물에 불린 쌀로 밥을 지어 밥 2공기를 준비한다.
2. 쇠고기는 채 썬 다음 배즙, 청주, 다진 파, 다진 마늘, 간장, 잣가루, 후춧가루, 참기름, 깨소금으로 양념한다.
3. 콩나물, 시금치나물, 애호박나물, 무나물, 도라지나물, 고사리나물, 취나물을 조금씩 준비한다. 표고버섯과 당근도 볶아서 준비한다. (p.18-21 참조)
4. 상추는 물에 씻어 물기를 털고 채 썬다. 김가루도 준비한다.
5. 돌솥에 고추기름을 두르고 밥을 담은 뒤 준비한 나물을 모두 올린다. 가운데 육회(쇠고기무침)를 얹고 그 위에 달걀노른자를 올린다.
6. 돌솥을 센 불에 올려서 달군 다음 밥을 담고 그 위에 모든 재료를 올려 양념고추장과 함께 상에 낸다.

Dolsot Bibimbap

A dolsot is a Korean traditional hot stone pot used to serve warm dishes. Dolsot Bibimbap is served in a sizzling hot dolsot with Namul, beef, and eggs.

Ingredients (2 servings)

2 bowls of cooked rice
2 leaves of lettuce
2Ts crushed dried seaweed
a little chili oil
2 egg yolks

Beef yukhoe

50g of beef, shred
a little bit of pear juice, rice wine, soy sauce, sesame oil, chopped leek, black pepper powder, crushed garlic, ground pine nuts and ground sesame

Seasoned vegetables (40g each)

bean sprouts, spinach, zucchini, radish, bellflower root, bracken, aster, Stir-fried Shiitake, Stir-fried carrot

Seasoned red pepper paste

3Ts red pepper paste
1Ts starch syrup
2ts plum extract, crushed garlic, sesame oil

Preparation

1. Prepare 2 bowls of cooked rice.
2. Shred beef and season with pear juice, rice wine, chopped leek, crushed garlic, soy sauce, ground pine nuts, ground pepper, sesame oil, and ground sesame.
3. Prepare seasoned bean sprouts, spinach, zucchini, bellflower root, radish, bracken, and aster. (see p.22-25)
4. Wash lettuce leaves, then remove water and shred them. Prepare crushed dried seaweed.
5. Grease dolsot with chili oil and put cooked rice in it. Place seasoned vegetables on top and place yukhoe in the middle. Place egg yolks on top.
6. Heat dolsot over high heat and serve with seasoned red pepper paste.

돼지고기김치볶음 비빔밥

잘 익은 김치와 돼지고기를 볶아서 따뜻한 밥에 나물과 함께 비벼 먹는 푸짐한 비빔밥

재료 (2인분)

밥 2공기

돼지고기김치볶음

돼지고기 50g
청주·생강즙 1작은술씩
김치 100g
양파·당근 ¼개씩
고추장·간장 1큰술씩
다진 마늘 1작은술
식용유 조금

각종 나물 (40g씩)

콩나물·시금치나물·도라지나물·
무나물·고사리나물

만드는 법

1. 물에 불린 쌀로 밥을 지어 밥 2공기를 준비한다.
2. 돼지고기는 먹기 좋게 썰어 청주, 생강즙으로 재운다.
3. 김치는 물기를 꼭 짠 후 잘게 썰고 양파, 당근은 채 썬다.
4. 팬에 기름을 두르고 ②의 돼지고기와 ③의 김치, 양파, 당근을 함께 넣어 볶는다. 고기가 조금 익으면 다진 마늘, 고추장, 간장으로 양념해 더 볶는다.
5. 콩나물, 시금치나물, 도라지나물, 무나물, 고사리나물을 조금씩 준비한다.
6. 그릇에 따뜻한 밥을 담고 준비한 나물과 돼지고기김치볶음을 보기 좋게 올린다.

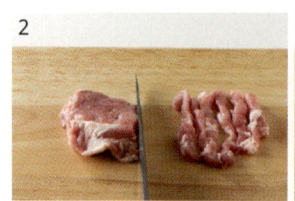

Fried Pork and Kimchi Bibimbap

This is a kind of Bibimbap that is served with fried pork, kimchi, warmed cooked rice and seasoned vegetables. It is also good to fry cooked rice.

Ingredients (2 servings)

2 bowls of cooked rice

Fried pork and kimchi
50g of pork
1ts rice wine
1ts ginger juice
100g of kimchi
¼ each of onion and carrot
1Ts red pepper paste
1Ts soy sauce
1ts chopped onion
a little cooking oil

Seasoned vegetables (40g each)
bean sprouts, spinach, radish, bellflower root, bracken

Preparation

1. Prepare 2 bowls of cooked rice.
2. Chop pork and soak it with rice wine and ginger juice.
3. Chop Kimchi, carrot and onion.
4. Pork of ② and kimchi, onion, and carrot of ③ and fry those together. When the meat is fried, season it with chopped onion, red pepper paste and soy sauce and fry them again.
5. Prepare each of the seasoned bean sprouts, spinach, bellflower root, radish, and bracken.
6. Put the warm cooked rice in a bowl and serve it with prepared seasoned vegetables and fried seasoned pork kimchi.

2
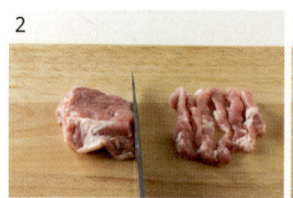

3

4

낙지 비빔밥

매콤한 낙지볶음이 입맛을 돌게 하는 비빔밥. 고춧가루를 가감해 맵기를 조절한다.

재료 (2인분)

밥 2공기
낙지 1마리
양파 ½개
미나리 60g
쑥갓 조금

식용유 2큰술

양념

간장·청주 1큰술씩
고춧가루·다진 마늘 1큰술씩
매실액·설탕 1큰술씩
참기름 ½큰술
생강즙 1작은술
통깨 조금

만드는 법

1 물에 불린 쌀로 밥을 지어 밥 2공기를 준비한다.
2 낙지는 내장을 제거하고 깨끗이 손질한다.
3 손질한 낙지는 끓는 물에 데쳐서 먹기 좋은 크기로 썬다.
4 미나리는 3cm 정도 길이로 썰고, 양파는 채 썬다.
5 팬에 기름을 두르고 뜨겁게 달군 뒤, 손질한 낙지와 통깨를 제외한 양념을 모두 넣고 볶는다. 미나리, 채 썬 양파를 넣고 조금 더 볶은 뒤 통깨를 뿌린다.
6 그릇에 따뜻한 밥을 담고 낙지볶음을 올린 후 쑥갓으로 장식한다.

Octopus Bibimbap

What is attractive about this varietyis the scent of octopus.
Use as much red pepper powder as one desires.

Ingredients (2 servings)

2 bowls of cooked rice
1 octopus
1 onion
60g of water parsley
a little crown daisy

2Ts cooking oil

Seasoning

1Ts soy sauce
1Ts rice wine
1Ts red pepper powder
1Ts sugar
1Ts chopped garlic
1Ts plum extract
½Ts sesame oil
1ts ginger juice
a little sesame

Preparation

1 Prepare 2 bowls of cooked rice.

2 Remove internal organs from the octopus.

3 Boil it in water and chop it in an appropriate size.

4 Chop up water parsley in about 3cm and also chop up onion.

5 Warm up the frying pan and fry octopus. Put water parsley, chopped onion and fry a little longer and sprinkle sesame.

6 Put warm cooked rice in a bowl and decorate it with crown daisy.

부추 비빔밥

부추와 콩나물, 무생채를 넣고 강된장에 비벼먹는 건강 비빔밥

재료 (2인분)

밥 2공기
콩나물 60g
무생채 60g
부추무침 60g
달걀노른자 2개

강된장

물 1컵
된장 1큰술
멸치가루 1작은술
청양고추 ½개
다진마늘 ½작은술
두부 50g

만드는 법

1. 콩나물을 삶아서 양념에 무쳐 준비한다. (p.18 참조)
2. 무를 채 썰어서 양념한 뒤 무생채를 준비한다. (p.19 참조)
3. 부추를 손질해 양념으로 무친다. (p.19 참조)
4. 물 1컵에 된장과, 멸치가루를 넣고 끓이다가 작게 자른 두부와 청양고추, 다진 마늘을 넣고 좀 더 끓여 강된장을 만든다.
5. 그릇에 따뜻한 밥을 담고 앞에서 준비한 콩나물, 무생채, 부추무침을 골고루 담는다. 가운데에 달걀노른자를 올리고 강된장을 넣어 비벼 먹는다.

Chive Bibimbap

A well-being Bibimbap dish with chives, bean sprouts, radish and seasoned soybean paste.

Ingredients (2 servings)

2 bowls of cooked rice
60g of Bean sprouts
60g of Spicy Radish Salad
60g of Chive Salad
2 egg yolks

Seasoned soybean paste

1Ts soybean paste
1 cup of water
1ts anchovy powder
½ hot pepper
½ts crushed garlic
50g of tofu

Preparation

1. Boil the bean sprouts and season. (see p.22)
2. Shred radish and season it for making spicy radish salad. (see p.23)
3. Cut chives into 5cm pieces and season. (see p.24)
4. Boil soybean paste and anchovy powder with water, then add chopped tofu, hot pepper, and crushed garlic for making seasoned soybean paste.
5. Prepare cooked rice and seasoned vegetables in a bowl. Place egg yolks in the middle and mix it with the soybeen paste.

1
2
3

꼬막 비빔밥

쫄깃하고 감칠맛 나는 꼬막은 봄이 제철. 봄 채소와 함께 초고추장에 비벼 먹으면 더 맛있다.

재료 (2인분)

밥 2공기
꼬막 200g
양파·청양고추 ½개씩
상추 5장
돌나물·새싹채소 50g씩
청주·김가루 조금씩

양념고추장

고추장 1½큰술
간장 1큰술
고춧가루·다진 마늘 ½큰술씩
올리고당·매실청 1큰술씩
설탕·식초 ½큰술씩
참기름 ½큰술
깨소금 1작은술
고추냉이 1작은술

만드는 법

1 꼬막은 소금물에 담가 해감을 뺀 뒤 박박 비벼 씻는다.
2 손질한 꼬막은 냄비에 물을 붓고 청주를 넣어 삶는다. 입이 벌어지면 건져서 꼬막살만 발라낸다.
3 양파는 가늘게 채 썰어 물에 담가두고 청양고추는 씻어서 송송 썬다. 상추와 돌나물, 새싹채소는 흐르는 물에 깨끗이 씻어 물기를 빼둔다.
4 밥을 그릇에 담고 그 위에 꼬막살과 채소, 김가루를 올린다.
5 양념고추장을 만들어 비벼 먹는다.

> **Tip** 꼬막을 너무 오래 익히면 질겨지고 육즙이 빠져나가 맛이 덜하다. 입이 살짝 벌어질 정도로만 익히면 된다.

Cockle Bibimbap

Cockles caught in Beolgyo are chewy and tasty. Enjoy the spring smell of bibimbap with cockles, veggies and seasoned red pepper paste.

Ingredients (2 servings)

2 bowls of cooked rice
200g of cockle
a little rice wine
½ onion
½ hot pepper
5 leaves of lettuce
50g of stonecrop
50g of vegetable sprout
a little seaweed flake

Seasoned red pepper paste

1½Ts red pepper paste
1Ts soy sauce
½Ts red pepper powder
½Ts crushed garlic
1Ts starch syrup
1Ts plum extract
1ts wasabi
½Ts sugar
½Ts vinegar
½Ts sesame oil
1ts ground sesame

Preparation

1. Soak cockles in salted water to remove sediment, then scrub them thoroughly.
2. Boil washed cockles with some rice wine. When the shells open, take out them and separate the meat.
3. Shred onion and soak it in cold water to remove spicy and chop washed hot pepper. Wash lettuces, stonecrops and vegetable sprouts, then squeeze out water.
4. Prepare cooked rice and put cockle meats, vegetables and seaweed flake in a bowl.
5. Make the seasoned red pepper paste and mix it with .

Tip Cockles should be cooked until shells are open slightly for the juicy and tender.

회생채 비빔밥

싱싱한 회와 아삭한 채소를 새콤달콤한 초고추장으로 비빈 비빔밥

재료 (2인분)

밥 2공기
참치회 50g, 레몬즙 ½큰술
오징어·문어 50g씩
쑥갓·깻잎·양배추 50g씩
당근·오이 50g씩
무순 20g
김 1장

초고추장

고추장·식초 2큰술씩
설탕·매실청 1큰술씩
다진 마늘 1작은술
생강즙 1작은술

만드는 법

1 물에 불린 쌀로 밥을 지어 밥 2공기를 준비한다.
2 참치회는 네모지게 썰어 레몬즙을 뿌려 둔다.
3 오징어와 문어는 살짝 데쳐서 먹기 좋은 크기로 썬다.
4 쑥갓과 깻잎, 양배추는 깨끗이 씻은 뒤 채 썬다. 당근과 오이는 채 썰고, 무순은 물에 씻은 뒤 물기를 털어 둔다.
5 김을 살짝 구워 손으로 잘게 부순다.
6 그릇에 밥을 담고 오징어와 문어, 채소, 무순, 김가루를 담은 뒤 가운데 참치회를 올린다.
7 초고추장을 만들어 비벼 먹는다.

Bibimbap with Sashimi

Bibimbap with fresh sashimi and vegetables.
It's sweet, sour and spicy, so it tastes very delicious.

Ingredients (2 servings)

2 bowls of cooked rice
50g of raw tuna sashimi
½Ts lemon juice
50g each of squid and octopus
50g each of crown daisy, sesame leaves and cabbage
50g each of carrot and cucumber
20g of radish sprouts
1 sheet of dried seaweed

Red pepper paste with vinegar

2Ts each of vinegar and red pepper paste
1Ts plum extract
1Ts sugar
1ts crushed garlic
1ts ginger juice

Preparation

1. Prepare 2 bowls of cooked rice.
2. Cut the raw tuna into rectangular pieces and sprinkle lemon juice.
3. Parboil squid and octopus and cut into bite-size pieces.
4. Wash crown daisy leaves, sesame leaves, and cabbage and shred them. Shred the carrots and cucumbers, wash the radish sprouts in water, and shake off the moisture.
5. Toast dried seaweed slightly and shred into tiny pieces.
6. Put the prepared portion of rice in a bowl with squid, octopus, vegetables, radish sprouts, and crushed dried seaweed. Place raw tuna sashimi in the middle.
7. Serve with red pepper paste with vinegar.

굴무밥

영양이 풍부한 굴과 무를 넣어 지은 따끈한 밥을 향긋한 달래간장에 비벼 먹는 비빔밥

재료 (2인분)

불린 쌀 2컵
굴 50g
무 ¼개
다시마국물 2컵
청주 2큰술

콩나물무침 80g
부추 80g

달래간장

다진 달래 2큰술
다진 마늘 1작은술
다진 풋고추 1작은술
간장 2큰술
고춧가루 2작은술
참기름 2작은술씩
깨소금 1작은술

만드는 법

1. 굴은 소금물에 헹구어 건져 놓는다.
2. 무는 껍질을 벗기고 채 썬다.
3. 돌솥에 채 썬 무를 깔고 불린 쌀을 얹은 다음, 다시마국물과 청주를 붓고 불에 올려 밥을 짓는다.
4. 밥이 되면 굴을 넣고 뜸을 푹 들인다.
5. 콩나물을 무쳐서 준비하고, 부추는 깨끗이 씻어 3~4cm 길이로 잘라 놓는다. (p.18-19 참조)
6. 밥이 다 되면 콩나물과 부추를 위에 올리고 달래간장에 비벼 먹는다.

Tip 콩나물은 굴과 함께 돌솥에 넣고 뜸을 들여도 좋다.

Oyster rice with Soy sauce

This is a kind of Bibimbap made with nutritious oyster and radish, seasoned with soy sauce.

Ingredients (2 servings)

Soaked rice 2 cups
50g of oyster
¼ radish
2 cups of kelp soup
2Ts rice wine

80g of seasoned bean sprouts
80g of chives

Wild chive soy sauce

2Ts chopped wild chive
1ts crushed garlic
1ts chopped green pepper
2Ts soy sauce
2ts red pepper powder
2ts sesame oil
1ts ground sesame

Preparation

1. Wash oyster in a salt water and take it out.
2. Peel out the skin of radish and chop it.
3. Put chopped radish at the bottom of pot, put soaked rice on it, and pour rice wine and kelp soup on it. Cook the rice.
4. When the rice of ③ is done, put oyster in and wait for enough time.
5. Prepare seasoned bean sprouts and washed chives, chop them in appropriate size. (see p.22)
6. When the rice is done, put bean sprouts and chives on rice and mix it with seasoned soy sauce.

> **Tip** Bean sprouts can be cooked in a stone pot with oysters.

양송이버섯 비빔밥

양송이버섯과 쇠고기, 양파, 달걀이 어우러진 달착지근하면서 부드러운 비빔밥

재료 (2인분)

밥 2공기

버섯볶음
양송이버섯 100g
올리브오일 1큰술
굴소스 2작은술

쇠고기 채소볶음
쇠고기 50g
달걀 2개
양파·애호박 ¼개씩
국간장 2큰술
설탕 1큰술
청주 ½큰술
다시마국물 1컵

만드는 법

1 물에 불린 쌀로 밥을 지어 밥 2공기를 준비한다.
2 양송이버섯은 끝을 잘라내고 길게 반 가른다.
3 쇠고기는 먹기 좋은 크기로 채 썬다. 양파와 애호박은 가늘게 채 썰어 놓는다.
4 팬에 올리브오일을 두르고 양송이버섯을 볶다가 굴소스를 넣어 간을 한다.
5 팬에 다시마국물, 국간장, 설탕, 청주를 끓이다가 쇠고기, 양파, 애호박을 넣어 익힌다. 고기가 익으면 달걀을 풀어 넣는다.
6 그릇에 따뜻한 밥을 담고 볶은 양송이버섯을 올린 후 ⑤의 쇠고기볶음을 끼얹는다.

Tip 양송이 대신 새송이나 표고 등 다른 버섯을 사용해도 좋다.

2

3

5

Mushroom Bibimbap

A soft and sweet Bibimbap that is in harmony with button mushroom, fried beef, onion and eggs.

Ingredients (2 servings)

2 bowls of cooked rice

Fried mushroom
100g of button mushroom
1Ts olive oil
2ts oyster sauce

Fried beef and vegetables
50g of beef
2 eggs
¼ onion
¼ zucchini
2Ts soy sauce
1Ts sugar
½Ts rice wine
1 cup of kelp soup

Preparation

1. Cook the rice and prepare 2 bowls of cooked rice.
2. Chop the end of button mushroom and cut it as half, long.
3. Cut beef in appropriate size. Chop onion and zucchini.
4. Put olive oil in frying pan and fry with mushrooms and season them with oyster sauce.
5. Put kelp soup, soy sauce, sugar, and rice wine in a frying pan and boil them. As nest, boil beef, onion, and zucchini. When the meat is done, put egg and boil it too.
6. Put warm cooked rice in a bowl, put fried white mushroom on it and also put fried seasoned beef of on it, too.

Tip You may use other mushrooms, such as birdsong or shiitake, instead of mushrooms.

2

3

5

우렁강된장 비빔밥

보리밥에 향긋한 삼색 나물을 얹은 후 구수하게 끓인 강된장으로 비벼 먹는 비빔밥

재료 (2인분)

보리밥 2공기
깻잎나물 50g
콩나물 50g
고사리나물 50g

우렁강된장

된장 1큰술
고추장 2작은술
양파·애호박 ¼개씩
다진 마늘 1작은술
풋고추 1작은술
새우가루 1큰술
우렁이 1큰술
멸치국물 1컵

만드는 법

1. 쌀과 보리쌀을 7:3으로 배합해 물에 충분히 불린 다음 밥을 짓는다.
2. 콩나물과 깻잎나물, 고사리나물을 조금씩 준비한다. (p.18-21 참조)
3. 강된장에 넣을 애호박과 양파는 굵게 다져 놓는다.
4. 뚝배기에 멸치국물을 넣고 된장과 고추장을 푼 다음 손질한 우렁이와 다진 애호박, 양파, 다진 마늘, 새우가루를 넣어 팔팔 끓인다.
5. 된장이 끓으면 다진 풋고추를 넣고 국물이 바짝 졸아들 때까지 더 끓인다.
6. 그릇에 따뜻한 보리밥을 담고 준비한 나물을 올린 다음 강된장을 함께 내서 비벼 먹는다.

2

2

5

Soybean paste Bibimbap

This is a kind of Bibimbap with cooked barely rice, sesame leaf, bracken and boiled soybean paste.

Ingredients (2 servings)

2 bowls of barely rice

Seasoned vegetables (50g each)
bean sprouts
bracken
sesame leaves

Seasoned soybean paste with mud snail
1Ts soybean paste
2ts red pepper paste
¼ onion
¼ zucchini
1ts crushed garlic
1ts chopped green pepper
1Ts shrimp powder
1Ts mud snail
1 cup of anchovy soup

Preparation

1. Cook barley and rice as the ratio of 7:3, soak them in water and cook them.

2. Prepare seasoned bean sprouts, seasoned bracken, and seasoned sesame leaves. (see p.22-25)

3. Chop zucchini and onion as a big size.

4. Put anchovy soup in a earthen pot and mix soybean paste and red pepper paste and put chopped zucchini, onion, crushed garlic, shrimp powder and mud snails. Boil them all.

5. When soybean sauce boils, put chopped green pepper and boil it until the amount of the soup is reduced.

6. Put warm cooked rice in a bowl, put seasoned vegetables on it and mix is with seasoned soybean paste.

Chapter 2

Fusion Bibimbap 퓨전 비빔밥

You can create varieties of Bibimbap. You can make pizza by sprinkling cheese on top of bibimbap, or you can stuff fried tofu with bibimbap. Here are some fusion Bibimbap dishes with a modern touch of flavor and presentation.

비빔밥을 이용해 다양한 음식을 만들 수 있다. 비빔밥 위에 치즈를 뿌려서 피자를 만들거나, 유부 등에 비빔밥으로 소를 채워 넣어도 좋다. 맛과 모양을 변화시킨 다양한 비빔밥을 만나 보자.

참치마요네즈 비빔밥

고소한 참치마요네즈 소스가 매운맛을 중화시키는 퓨전 비빔밥

재료 (2인분)

기본 비빔밥
밥 2공기
나물 또는 채소 적당량
고추장 3큰술
물엿 ½큰술
참기름 조금

붉은 고추(또는 올리브) 조금
달걀 1개

참치마요네즈 소스
참치통조림 2큰술
마요네즈 2큰술
다진 오이피클 1큰술
다진 양파 1큰술
된장 1큰술
레몬즙 1작은술
설탕 ½큰술
식초 ½큰술
소금 조금

만드는 법

1. 따뜻한 밥에 채소, 나물 등 있는 재료를 다져 넣고 고추장, 물엿, 참기름으로 비벼서 기본 비빔밥을 만든다.
2. 참치통조림의 기름기를 꼭 짠 후 레몬즙을 조금 뿌린다. 다진 양파는 설탕과 식초에 잠시 절인 후 물기를 꼭 짠다.
3. 기름 뺀 참치와 절인 양파, 다진 오이피클, 마요네즈, 된장을 한데 섞어 참치마요네즈 소스를 만든다.
4. 달걀을 삶아 노른자만 따로 으깬다.
5. 비빔밥을 한 숟가락 떠서 머핀 틀이나 작은 그릇에 담는다.
6. 밥 위에 참치마요네즈 소스를 얹고 달걀노른자 가루를 뿌린 다음 붉은 고추 또는 올리브로 장식한다.

Tuna Mayonnaise Bibimbap

This fusion dish has tuna mayonnaise sauce to cover the spiciness of Bibimbap, making it unique.

Ingredients (2 servings)

Basic bibimbap
2 bowls of cooked rice
enough Namul or herbs
3Ts red pepper paste
½Ts starch syrup
a little sesame oil

a little red pepper
(or black olives)
1 egg

Tuna mayonnaise sauce
2Ts canned tuna
2Ts mayonnaise
1Ts chopped onions
1Ts chopped cucumber pickles
1Ts soybean paste
1ts lemon juice
½Ts sugar
½Ts vinegar
a little salt

Preparation

1. Make basic bibimbap by putting chopped Namul(seasoned vegetable) or herbs in warm rice and mixing it with red pepper paste, starch syrup and sesame oil.

2. Squeeze out oil from canned tuna and sprinkle some lemon juice. Pickle chopped onion in vinegar and sugar for a while. Then squeeze out moisture.

3. Mix tuna, pickled onion, chopped pickles, mayonnaise, and soybean paste to make tuna mayonnaise sauce.

4. Boil an egg. Separate the yolk from the white and mash it.

5. Put a spoonful of Bibimbap in a muffin cup or on a small plate.

6. Place the tuna mayonnaise sauce on top of the prepared Bibimbap. Sprinkle mashed egg yolk on top and garnish with red pepper or black olives.

비빔밥 피자

밀가루로 만든 피자도우 대신 비빔밥을 누룽지처럼 구운 한국식 피자

재료 (2인분)

기본 비빔밥
밥 2공기
나물 또는 채소 적당량
고추장 3큰술
물엿 ½큰술
참기름 조금

피자치즈 1컵
블랙 올리브·양송이버섯 2개씩
양파·청피망·홍피망 ¼개씩
식용유·파슬리가루 조금씩

피자소스
다진 쇠고기 ½컵
토마토케첩 3큰술
고추장·물 2큰술씩
물엿 1큰술
다진 파 1큰술
다진 마늘 ½큰술
청주·설탕·참기름 ½큰술씩
생강즙 2작은술

만드는 법

1. 따뜻한 밥에 채소, 나물 등 있는 재료를 다져 넣고 고추장, 물엿, 참기름으로 비벼서 기본 비빔밥을 만든다.
2. 팬에 참기름을 두르고 다진 쇠고기, 다진 마늘, 고추장, 토마토케첩, 청주를 넣어 볶는다. 여기에 다진 파, 생강즙, 설탕, 물엿, 물을 넣고 끓여 피자소스를 만든다.
3. 팬에 식용유를 조금 두르고 비빔밥을 얇게 펼친 뒤 약간 딱딱해질 정도로 굽는다.
4. 구운 밥에 피자소스를 바르고 올리브, 양송이버섯, 양파, 피망을 슬라이스 해서 올린 다음 피자치즈를 뿌린다.
5. 뚜껑을 덮고 약한 불에서 익힌다. 치즈가 녹으면 파슬리 가루를 골고루 뿌린다.

Bibimbap Pizza

This Korean-style pizza uses pan-fried Bibimbap dough instead of the original flour dough.

Ingredients (2 servings)

Basic bibimbap
2 bowls of cooked rice
enough Namul or herbs
3Ts red pepper paste
½Ts starch syrup
a little sesame oil

1 cup of pizza cheese
2 black olives
2 button mushrooms
¼ green and red bell pepper
¼ onion
a little bit of cooking oil
and chopped parsley

Pizza sauce
½ cup of minced beef
3Ts tomato ketchup
2Ts of red pepper paste, water
1Ts starch syrup
1Ts chopped leek
½Ts each of crushed garlic, rice wine, sugar, sesame oil
2ts ginger juice

Preparation

1. Make basic bibimbap by putting chopped Namul(seasoned vegetable) or herbs in warm rice and mixing it with red pepper paste, starch syrup and sesame oil.

2. Grease the frying pan with sesame oil and stir-fry minced beef with crushed garlic, red pepper paste, tomato ketchup, and rice wine.

3. Grease another pan with cooking oil. Spread out the prepared portion of Bibimbap thinly and pan-fry until it becomes slightly hard.

4. Spread the pizza sauce on the pan-fried Bibimbap dough. Place sliced black olives, button mushrooms, onions, and bell peppers on the Bibimbap and sprinkle shredded pizza cheese over it.

5. Cover the pan with a lid and let the pizza cook over a low heat. Once the cheese melts, sprinkle chopped parsley and serve.

1

3

4

5

비빔밥 크레이프

크레이프로 비빔밥을 돌돌 말아 한 입에 쏙 먹기 좋은 핑거 푸드를 만들었다.

재료 (2인분)

기본 비빔밥
밥 2공기
나물 또는 채소 적당량
고추장 3큰술
물엿 ½큰술
참기름 조금

우유 1컵
달걀 2개
밀가루 5큰술
설탕 1큰술
버터 1큰술
식용유 조금

두부크림 소스
두부 ½모
두유 3큰술
꿀 2큰술
레몬즙 1큰술
소금 조금

만드는 법

1 따뜻한 밥에 채소, 나물 등 있는 재료를 다져 넣고 고추장, 물엿, 참기름으로 비벼서 기본 비빔밥을 만든다.
2 달걀을 푼 다음 우유, 설탕을 넣고 섞는다. 여기에 밀가루와 녹인 버터를 넣고 섞어 크레이프 반죽을 만든다.
3 팬에 식용유를 두르고 반죽을 떠넣어 동그랗고 얇게 크레이프를 부친다.
4 두부와 꿀, 두유, 레몬즙, 소금을 믹서에 함께 넣고 곱게 갈아 두부크림 소스를 만든다.
5 크레이프 위에 비빔밥을 한 숟가락 얹어 돌돌 말아준다.
6 크레이프 롤을 접시에 담고 두부크림 소스를 곁들인다.

Bibimbap Crepes

Bibimbap can be rolled in crepes, making perfect bite-size finger food.

Ingredients (2 servings)

Basic bibimbap
2 bowls of cooked rice
enough Namul or herbs
3Ts red pepper paste
½Ts starch syrup
a little sesame oil

1 cup of milk
2 eggs
5Ts flour
1Ts sugar
1Ts butter
a little cooking oil

Tofu cream sauce
½ block of tofu
3Ts soy milk
2Ts honey
1Ts lemon juice
a little salt

Preparation

1. Make basic bibimbap by putting chopped Namul(seasoned vegetable) or herbs in warm rice and mixing it with red pepper paste, starch syrup and sesame oil.

2. Whip eggs and add milk and sugar. Add flour and melted butter to make batter.

3. Grease the pan and pour batter. Spread the batter thinly and shape it as it cooks.

4. Use a mixer to grind tofu, honey, lemon juice, and salt.

5. Place a spoonful of Bibimbap on the crepe and roll it up.

6. Place the crepes and serve with tofu cream sauce.

떡갈비 비빔밥

쇠고기를 잘게 다져서 양념한 후 비빔밥과 함께 동글게 빚어 구운 한국식 미트볼

재료 (2인분)

기본 비빔밥
밥 2공기
나물 또는 채소 적당량
고추장 3큰술
물엿 ½큰술
참기름 조금

김치 조금

떡갈비
쇠고기 갈비살 200g
다진 양파 ½컵
다진 파·다진 마늘 1큰술씩
간장 1큰술
배즙 3큰술
설탕 2큰술
생강즙 1작은술
청주 4작은술씩
소금·후춧가루·참기름 조금씩

만드는 법

1. 따뜻한 밥에 채소, 나물 등 있는 재료를 다져 넣고 고추장, 물엿, 참기름으로 비벼서 기본 비빔밥을 만든다.
2. 쇠고기 갈비살은 다져 놓는다.
3. 다진 양파, 다진 파, 다진 마늘, 간장, 배즙, 생강즙, 청주, 설탕, 소금, 후춧가루, 참기름을 섞어서 고기 양념을 만든다.
4. ③의 고기 양념을 다진 쇠고기와 섞어 1시간 정도 재운다.
5. ①의 기본 비빔밥에 양념한 쇠고기를 섞어 동글납작하게 떡갈비를 빚는다.
6. 팬에 기름을 두르고 ⑤를 올려 앞뒤로 뒤집어가며 굽는다.

1

4

5

6

Bibimbap Tteokgalbi

Tteokgalbi is Korean-style meatballs-shaped Bibimbap with ground marinated beef ribs.

Ingredients (2 servings)

Basic bibimbap
2 bowls of cooked rice
enough Namul or herbs
3Ts red pepper paste
½Ts starch syrup
a little sesame oil

a little kimchi

Tteokgalbi
200g of beef ribs
½ cup of chopped onions
1Ts chopped leek
1Ts crushed garlic
1Ts soy sauce
3Ts pear juice
2Ts sugar
4ts rice wine
1ts ginger juice
a little bit of salt,
ground pepper,
and sesame oil

Preparation

1. Make basic bibimbap by putting chopped Namul(seasoned vegetable) or herbs in warm rice and mixing it with red pepper paste, starch syrup and sesame oil.

2. Mince the beef.

3. Mix chopped onions, chopped leek, crushed garlic, soy sauce, pear juice, ginger juice, rice wine, sugar, salt, ground pepper, and sesame oil to make a marinade.

4. Pour ③ over minced beef and marinate it for an hour.

5. Mix the marinated beef and basic bibimbap of ①, then shape the mixture into round, flat tteokgalbi portions.

6. Cook in a frying pan with oil. Flip them every once in a while as they cook.

1

4

5

6

유부 비빔밥

여러 가지 나물과 채소로 비빔밥을 만들어 유부 속에 채워 넣은 한 입 밥

재료 (2인분)

기본 비빔밥
밥 2공기
나물 또는 채소 적당량
고추장 3큰술
물엿 ½큰술
참기름 조금

유부 8장

양념간장
간장·다시마국물 2큰술씩
물엿 ½큰술
청주 ½작은술
매실액 1작은술
깨소금·참기름 1작은술씩

만드는 법

1. 따뜻한 밥에 채소, 나물 등 있는 재료를 다져 넣고 고추장, 물엿, 참기름으로 비벼서 기본 비빔밥을 만든다.
2. 팬에 ①의 비빔밥을 넣고 보슬보슬하게 볶는다.
3. 유부는 물기를 꼭 짠다.
4. 유부 속에 볶은 비빔밥을 꼭꼭 눌러가며 담아 속을 채운다.
5. 유부비빔밥을 접시에 담고 양념간장을 만들어 찍어 먹는다.

Fried Tofu Bibimbap

Fried Tofu Bibimbap has mixed vegetables, and stuff the fried tofu by filling it with rice.

Ingredients (2 servings)

Basic bibimbap
2 bowls of cooked rice
enough Namul or herbs
3Ts red pepper paste
½Ts starch syrup
a little sesame oil

8 sheet of fried tofu

Soy sauce
2Ts soy bean
2Ts kelp soup
½Ts starch syrup
½ts rice wine
1ts plum extract
1ts each of sesame oil and ground sesame

Preparation

1. Make basic bibimbap by putting chopped Namul(seasoned vegetable) or herbs in warm rice and mixing it with red pepper paste, starch syrup and sesame oil.
2. Put Bibimbap in the frying pan with Bibimbap of ① and boil it down without moist.
3. Drain fried tofu.
4. Stuff the fried tofu with stir-fried bibimbap inside.
5. Place Fried Tofu Bibimbap on a plate and serve it with seasoned soy sauce.

찹쌀고기말이 비빔밥

얇게 저민 쇠고기로 비빔밥을 돌돌 말아 겨자간장에 찍어 먹는 일품요리

재료 (2인분)

기본 비빔밥
밥 2공기
나물 또는 채소 적당량
고추장 3큰술
물엿 ½큰술
참기름 조금

쇠고기 찹쌀구이
쇠고기 200g
찹쌀가루 ½컵
간장 3큰술
설탕·배즙 2큰술씩
청주 1큰술
다진 파 1큰술
다진 마늘 ½큰술
후춧가루·식용유 조금씩

겨자간장
겨자 1큰술
간장·식초·설탕 2큰술씩

만드는 법

1 따뜻한 밥에 채소, 나물 등 있는 재료를 다져 넣고 고추장, 물엿, 참기름으로 비벼서 기본 비빔밥을 만든다.
2 얇게 슬라이스 한 쇠고기에 다진 파, 다진 마늘, 간장, 설탕, 배즙, 청주, 후춧가루를 넣고 무쳐서 30분 정도 둔다.
3 양념한 쇠고기에 찹쌀가루를 앞뒷면에 묻힌 다음 기름 두른 팬에 굽는다.
4 ①의 기본 비빔밥을 손으로 뭉친 다음 구운 쇠고기 위에 올려 돌돌 만다.
5 흐트러지지 않도록 꼬치를 끼운 다음 접시에 담아 겨자간장과 함께 낸다.

1

2

3

5

Bibimbap Beef Roll

In this Bibimbap variety, Bibimbap is rolled with thinly sliced beef, and is to be dipped in mustard soy sauce.

Ingredients (2 servings)

Basic bibimbap
2 bowls of cooked rice
enough Namul or herbs
3Ts red pepper paste
½Ts starch syrup
a little sesame oil

Grilled beef with glutinous rice
200g of beef
½ cup of glutinous rice
3TS soy sauce
2Ts sugar
2Ts pear juice
1Ts rice wine
1Ts chopped leek
½Ts crushed garlic
a little ground pepper and cooking oil

Mustard soy sauce
1Ts mustard
2Ts soy sauce
2Ts vinegar
2Ts sugar

Preparation

1. Make basic bibimbap by putting chopped Namul(seasoned vegetable) or herbs in warm rice and mixing it with red pepper paste, starch syrup and sesame oil.
2. Put chopped leek, crushed garlic, soy sauce, sugar, pear juice, rice wine, and ground pepper on thin sliced beef and marinate it for 30 minutes.
3. Coat beef from ② with ground glutinous rice, grease the frying pan, and grill it.
4. Hold together Bibimbap from ① with your hands and roll it with grilled beef.
5. Make it fixed with skewers and serve it on a dish with mustard soy sauce.

1
2
3
5

비빔밥 옥수수전

옥수수와 김치, 각종 채소를 다져 비빔밥을 만든 후 동글납작하게 빚어서 지진 전

재료 (2인분)

밥 1공기
김치 80g
브로콜리·파프리카 30g씩
양파·당근 30g씩
옥수수 통조림 2큰술
다진 파·마늘 2작은술씩
참기름 2작은술
달걀 2개
밀가루 ½컵
소금 조금
식용유 적당량

양념간장

간장 2큰술
배즙·식초 1큰술씩
양파즙 2작은술
연겨자 1작은술
소금·후춧가루 조금씩

만드는 법

1 물에 불린 쌀로 밥을 지어 밥 1공기를 준비한다. 옥수수 통조림은 체에 건진다.
2 잘 익은 김치를 준비해 잘게 다져서 물기를 꼭 짠다.
3 브로콜리와 파프리카, 양파, 당근을 잘게 다져서 기름 두른 팬에 볶는다. 다진 파, 다진 마늘, 소금을 넣고 맛을 낸다.
4 따뜻한 밥에 ③의 볶은 재료와 옥수수, 참기름을 넣고 섞은 다음 밀가루, 달걀을 풀어 넣고 반죽을 한다.
5 달군 팬에 기름을 두르고 ④의 반죽을 올려 동글게 모양을 잡아가며 익힌다.
6 양념간장을 만들어 김치비빔밥 전과 함께 내서 찍어 먹는다.

Bibimbap Pancake

This is Bibimbap with minced corns, kimchi and other vegetables and then grilled in a flat shape.

Ingredients (2 servings)

1 bowl of cooked rice
80g of kimchi
30g each of broccoli, onions, paprika, carrots
2Ts canned corn
2ts crushed garlic
2ts chopped leek
2ts sesame oil
2 eggs
½ cup of flour
a little salt and cooking oil

Seasoning soy sauce

2Ts soy sauce
1Ts pear juice
1Ts vinegar
2ts onion juice
1ts soft mustard
a little salt and ground pepper

Preparation

1. Cook rice that has been soaked in water for a while to prepare 1 bowl of cooked rice. Dehydrate canned corns with a sifter.

2. Prepare fermented sour kimchi, mince it, and then squeeze it for dehydration.

3. Mince broccoli, paprika, onions and carrots, and put chopped leek, crushed garlic, and salt and fry them together.

4. Put and mix together warm cooked rice, kimchi, broccoli, paprika, onions, carrots, corns, and sesame oil. Put flour and stirred eggs and make paste.

5. Grease heated frying pan and put paste from ④ and make circular shape throughout grilling.

6. Make seasoning soy sauce and serve kimchi Bibimbap pancake with the sauce as dipping sauce.

비빔밥 크로켓

비빔밥 속에 치즈를 넣고 바삭하게 튀긴 크로켓. 고소한 땅콩버터 간장소스가 잘 어울린다.

재료 (2인분)

기본 비빔밥
밥 2공기
나물 또는 채소 적당량
고추장 3큰술
물엿 ½큰술
참기름 조금

크로켓
모차렐라 치즈 6큰술
빵가루 4큰술
밀가루 2큰술
달걀 2개
식용유 적당량

땅콩버터 간장소스
간장 2큰술
땅콩버터·꿀 1큰술
레몬즙 ½큰술
검은깨 1작은술

만드는 법

1. 따뜻한 밥에 채소, 나물 등 있는 재료를 다져 넣고 고추장, 물엿, 참기름으로 비벼서 기본 비빔밥을 만든다.
2. 기본 비빔밥으로 주먹밥을 빚은 후 속에 모차렐라 치즈를 1작은술 넣고 오므린다.
3. ②에 밀가루를 묻히고 달걀물을 입힌 다음 빵가루를 묻힌다.
4. 160℃로 끓는 기름에 ③을 넣어 튀긴다.
5. 땅콩버터 간장소스를 만들어 곁들여 낸다.

Bibimbap Croquette

Crispy fried Bibimbap added mozzarella cheese.
The soft cheese and savory peanut butter soy sauce go well.

Ingredients (2 servings)

Basic bibimbap
2 bowls of cooked rice
enough Namul or herbs
3Ts red pepper paste
½Ts starch syrup
a little sesame oil

Croquette
6Ts mozzarella cheese
4Ts bread crumbs
2Ts flour
2 eggs
enough cooking oil

Peanut butter soy sauce
2Ts soy sauce
1Ts honey
1Ts peanut butter
½Ts lemon juice
1ts black sesame

Preparation

1. Make basic bibimbap by putting chopped Namul(seasoned vegetable) or herbs in warm rice and mixing it with red pepper paste, starch syrup and sesame oil.

2. Place basic bibimbap a handful on your hand and put 1ts mozzarella cheese, then make them round.

3. Coat ② with flour, then dip them in whipped egg and roll them in bread crumbs.

4. Fry ③ in oil boiling at 160℃.

5. Make peanut butter soy sauce and serve it with the croquette.

1

3

4

5

잡곡 비빔밥 케이크

색색의 잡곡밥을 쌓아 케이크처럼 만들었다. 모양도 예쁘고 맛도 좋은 영양만점 비빔밥

재료 (2인분)

달걀노른자 1개
잣 5개
당근 ¼개

잡곡밥

쌀 1½컵
좁쌀·검은쌀·팥 ½컵씩

각종 나물 (30g씩)

콩나물·시금치나물·
도라지나물·고사리나물

볶음고추장

다진 쇠고기 2큰술
고추장·물 2큰술씩
청주·설탕 ½큰술씩
참기름·깨소금 ½큰술씩
다진 마늘 ½큰술
물엿·다진 생강 ½작은술씩

만드는 법

1. 검은쌀밥, 좁쌀밥, 팥밥 등 3가지 색의 밥을 짓는다. 검은쌀과 좁쌀은 각각 쌀 ½컵과 섞어서 물에 불렸다가 밥을 짓고, 팥은 한나절 정도 물에 불렸다가 삶아 쌀 ½컵과 섞어 밥을 짓는다.

2. 콩나물·시금치나물·도라지나물·고사리나물을 준비해 잘게 다진다. 당근볶음도 잘게 다져서 준비한다. (p.18-21 참조)

3. 지름 7~10cm 정도의 둥근 틀에 검은쌀밥을 넣고 눌러 둥글 납작하게 만든다. 좁쌀밥과 팥밥도 똑같이 만든다.

4. 볶음고추장 재료를 볶아 볶음고추장을 만든다.

5. ③에서 만든 팥밥 위에 콩나물·시금치나물을 올린 후 볶음고추장을 바른다.

6. ⑤ 위에 조밥을 얹고 볶은 당근·도라지나물·고사리나물을 올린 후 볶음고추장을 바른다.

7. ⑥ 위에 검은쌀밥을 얹고 채 썬 달걀지단과 잣을 올린다.

Multigrain Bibimbap Cake

A nutritious bibimbap that colorful multigrain rice is stacked like a cake looks beautiful and tastes good.

Ingredients (2 servings)

1 egg yolk
5 pine nuts
¼ carrot

Cooked rice with multigrain
1½ cups of rice
½ cup each of millet,
black rice and red bean

Seasoned vegetables (30g each)
bean sprouts, spinach,
bellflower roots, bracken

Stir-fried red pepper paste
2Ts each of red pepper paste,
minced beef and water
½Ts each of rice wine, sesame oil, crushed garlic, sugar and ground sesame
½ts each of starch syrup and crushed ginger

Preparation

1. Mix black rice and millet with ½ cup each of rice, then soak in water before cooking. Red beans are soaked in water for about 12 hour, then cook it mixed with ½ cup of rice.

2. Chop each of the seasoned bean sprouts, spinach, bellflower roots and bracken. Shred the carrots and sauté it with a dash of salt. (see p.22-25)

3. Place cooked black rice into a round frame about 7~10cm in diameter and press it to flat.

4. Sauté the ingredients for making stir-fried red pepper paste.

5. Place seasoned bean sprouts and spinach on ③, then spread stir-fried red pepper paste.

6. Place cooked millet on ⑤, then put on stir-fried carrot, seasoned bellflower roots and bracken too. And spread stir-fried red pepper paste.

7. Place cooked black rice on ⑥, then place cooked egg slices and pine nut.

비빔 꼬마김밥

고추장에 비빈 밥을 무순, 오이피클, 단무지와 함께 돌돌 말아 한 입에 먹기 간편한 김밥

재료 (2인분)

기본 비빔밥
밥 2공기
나물 또는 채소 적당량
고추장 3큰술
물엿 ½큰술
참기름 조금

김 4장
오이피클 4개
단무지 4개
당근 ¼개
무순 20g

만드는 법

1 따뜻한 밥에 채소, 나물 등 있는 재료를 다져 넣고 고추장, 물엿, 참기름으로 비벼서 기본 비빔밥을 만든다.
2 김은 살짝 구워서 4등분으로 나눈다.
3 오이피클과 단무지는 5cm 길이로 잘라 굵게 채 썰고, 당근도 같은 길이로 잘라 채 썬다.
4 김발에 구운 김을 놓고 ①의 기본 비빔밥을 얇게 올린 후 채 썬 오이피클, 단무지, 당근, 무순을 얹어 돌돌 만다.
5 김밥을 먹기 좋은 크기로 썰어 도시락에 예쁘게 담는다.

Little Gimbap with Bibimbap

This is a rolled Gimbap with Bibimbap, radish sprout, pickled cucumber, pickled radish. It is more convenient to eat Bibimbap rolled in Gimbap.

Ingredients (2 servings)

Basic bibimbap
2 bowls of cooked rice
enough Namul or herbs
3Ts red pepper paste
½Ts starch syrup
a little sesame oil

4 sheets of dried seaweed
4 pieces of cucumber pickle
4 pieces of radish pickle
¼ carrot
20g of radish sprout

Preparation

1. Make basic bibimbap by putting chopped Namul(seasoned vegetable) or herbs in warm rice and mixing it with red pepper paste, starch syrup and sesame oil.

2. Toast the dried seaweed lightly and divide into four parts.

3. Cut pickled cucumber and pickled radish in 5cm and cut the carrots in the same length.

4. Place the dried seaweed on Gimbap blind and put on basic Bibimbap thinly, then put on pickled cucumber, pickled radish, carrot, radish sprout and roll.

5. Present Gimbap in bite-size and put it in lunch box.

Chapter 3

Bibimbap for dieting 다이어트 비빔밥

This Bibimbap variety is well-balanced in nutrition with mixed vegetables and meat. Low in calorie, Bibimbap will not likely be fattening. Let's set up a healthy table with Bibimbap, which is good for dieting.

비빔밥은 한 그릇에 여러 가지 채소와 고기가 들어가 영양의 균형이 잘 잡혀 있다. 칼로리가 적어서 아무리 많이 먹어도 살이 찌지 않는다. 다이어트에 좋은 비빔밥으로 건강한 식탁을 차려보자.

산채 비빔밥

비타민, 미네랄이 풍부한 여러 가지 산나물을 넣고 고추장에 쓱쓱 비벼 먹는 건강 비빔밥

재료 (2인분)

현미밥 2공기

쇠고기볶음

다진 쇠고기 50g
다진 파·다진 마늘·간장·설탕·
깨소금·참기름·후춧가루 조금씩

각종 나물 (40g씩)

도라지나물·시래기나물·취나물·
깻잎나물·냉이나물·달래무침
당근볶음·표고버섯볶음

양념고추장

고추장 2큰술
된장 1큰술
물엿 1큰술
다진 파 1큰술
다진 마늘·참기름 2작은술씩
깨소금 1작은술

만드는 법

1. 현미를 물에 충분히 불려 밥을 짓는다.
2. 다진 쇠고기는 다진 파, 다진 마늘, 간장, 설탕, 참기름, 깨소금, 후춧가루로 양념해서 팬에 볶는다.
3. 도라지나물, 시래기나물, 취나물, 깻잎나물을 준비한다. (p.20-21 참조)
4. 냉이는 된장으로 무친 냉이된장나물을 준비한다. (p.19 참조)
5. 당근과 표고버섯은 채 썰어 볶아둔다. (p.21 참조)
6. 그릇에 현미밥을 담고 준비한 나물과 당근·버섯 볶은 것을 빙 둘러 담는다. 그런 다음 가운데에 쇠고기 볶은 것을 올린다.
7. 양념고추장을 만들어 비벼 먹는다.

Sanchae Bibimbap

Sanchae Bibimbap mixes an assortment of fresh greens, rich in vitamins and minerals, in red pepper paste.

Ingredients (2 servings)

2 bowls of cooked brown rice

Bulgogi
50g of chopped beef
a little bit of pepper, sugar
chopped leek, sesame oil,
crushed garlic, soy sauce,
and ground sesame

Seasoned vegetables (40g each)
bellflower root,
dried radish leaves,
aster, sesame leaves,
shepherd's purse,
wild chive, carrot, shiitake

Seasoning red pepper paste
2Ts red pepper paste
1Ts soybean paste
1Ts starch syrup
1Ts chopped leek
2ts crushed garlic
2ts sesame oil
1ts ground sesame

Preparation

1 Cook brown rice after being soaked in water.

2 Season the meat with chopped leek, crushed garlic, soy sauce, sugar, sesame oil, ground sesame and pepper, then sauté them.

3 Blanch and season bellflower root, dried radish leaves, aster, sesame leaves. (see p.24-25)

4 Prepare shepherd's purse by seasoned it with soybean paste. (see p.23)

5 Fry shredded carrot and shiitake with a little bit of salt. (see p.25)

6 Put cooked rice in a bowl and also place the prepared Seasoned vegetables, sautéed carrots and shiitake in a circular manner. Beef should be placed in the middle.

7 Mix with the seasoned red pepper paste and serve.

3

4

5

채소샐러드 비빔밥

여러 가지 신선한 채소에 상큼한 사과간장 소스를 곁들어 샐러드처럼 즐기는 비빔밥

재료 (2인분)

현미밥 2공기
간장 2큰술
후리가케·김가루 1큰술씩
참기름 1큰술
양배추·적양배추 50g씩
양상추·오이 50g씩
달걀 2개

사과간장 소스

사과즙 2큰술
간장 3큰술
양파즙·당근즙 1큰술씩
설탕·청주 1큰술씩
올리브오일 1큰술
깨소금 2작은술

만드는 법

1. 양배추, 적양배추, 오이는 채 썰고 양상추는 적당한 크기로 뜯는다.
2. 달걀은 삶아서 노른자만 곱게 부순다.
3. 따뜻한 현미밥에 간장, 후리가케, 김가루, 참기름을 넣어 고루 섞는다.
4. 그릇에 양념한 밥을 담고 준비한 샐러드 채소를 올린 후 달걀노른자 가루를 뿌린다.
5. 사과간장 소스를 만들어 함께 채소샐러드 비빔밥에 넣고 비벼 먹는다.

1

2

3

Vegetable salad Bibimbap

Bibimbap with fresh apple soy sauce on various fresh vegetables and enjoying it like a salad.

Ingredients (2 servings)

2 bowls of cooked brown rice
2Ts soy sauce
1Ts seaweed flake
1Ts Hurigake
1Ts sesame oil
50g of cabbage
50g of red cabbage
50g of lead lettuce
50g of cucumber
2 eggs

Apple-soybean sauce

3Ts soy sauce
2Ts apple juice
1Ts onion juice
1Ts carrot juice
1Ts sugar
1Ts rice wine
1Ts olive oil
2ts ground sesame

Preparation

1 Shred cabbage, red cabbage and cucumber and pull out head lettuce in appropriate size.

2 Boil eggs and crush only yolks.

3 Mix soy sauce, Hurigake, seaweed flake and sesame oil with warm cooked brown rice.

4 Put seasoned rice in a bowl, with prepared vegetable salad and sprinkle yolk powder.

5 Mix Bibimbap with apple-soybean sauce and serve.

단호박 비빔밥

단호박 속에 잡곡을 넣고 솥밥처럼 찜을 해서 열무김치를 곁들여 먹는 비빔밥

재료 (2인분)

단호박 2개
열무김치 100g
채 썬 양배추·무순 40g씩
달걀 1개

잡곡밥

현미 찹쌀 2컵
쌀·검은쌀·팥·조·검은콩 2큰술씩
은행 조금

강된장찌개

으깬 두부 2큰술
다진 파 1큰술
다진 마늘 1작은술
된장 1큰술
고추장 ½큰술
참기름 1작은술
쌀뜨물 1컵

만드는 법

1 팥은 삶고, 현미 찹쌀·검은쌀·검은콩은 3시간 정도 물에 불린다. 쌀과 좁쌀은 30분 정도 불린다.
2 단호박은 꼭지 부분을 가로로 자르고 씨는 모두 긁어낸다.
3 단호박 안에 불린 잡곡과 팥, 은행을 넣고 쌀이 잠길 정도로 물을 붓는다.
4 잘라둔 단호박 꼭지 부분으로 뚜껑을 덮은 뒤 찜통에 올려서 20분간 찐다.
5 달걀을 곱게 푼 뒤 얇게 부쳐서 채 썬다.
6 쌀뜨물에 된장과 고추장을 풀고 으깬 두부, 다진 파, 다진 마늘, 참기름을 넣어 강된장찌개를 끓인다.
7 단호박밥 위에 열무김치와 채소, 달걀 채 썬 것, 무순을 돌려가며 담은 뒤 강된장과 함께 내서 비벼 먹는다.

Pumpkin Bibimbap

This Bibimbap is made with multigrain rice and pumpkin.
Serve with yeolmu kimchi(young radish kimchi).

Ingredients (2 servings)

2 Pumpkins
100g of yeolmu kimchi
40g of chopped cabbage
40g of radish sprout
1 egg

Cooked rice with multigrain

2 cups of brown rice
2Ts each of rice, black rice, red bean, millet and black bean, a little ginkgo nut

Soybean sauce soup

2Ts crushed tofu
1Ts chopped leek
1ts crushed garlic
1Ts soybeen paste
½Ts red pepper paste
1ts sesame oil
1 cup of rice water

Preparation

1. Boil red bean, soak brown rice, black rice, and black beans for about 3 hours in water. Soak rice and millet in water for about 30 minutes.
2. Cut the stalk of pumpkin across and get all the seeds out.
3. Place the grains, red bean and gingko nuts in the pumpkin and pour everything is soaked.
4. Place the pumpkin stalk as a cover and steam it in a steamer.
5. Whip the egg. Pan-fry it and thinly slice it.
6. Mix soybean sauce and red pepper paste with rice water and boil it with crushed tofu, chopped leek, crushed garlic and sesame oil.
7. Place yeolmu kimchi, sliced egg, radish sprout in circle on top of the pumpkin rice and serve it with the soybean sauce soup.

콩나물 비빔밥

콩나물과 표고버섯, 당근 볶은 것을 올리고 향긋한 달래간장으로 비벼 먹는 콩나물밥

재료 (2인분)

콩나물밥
불린 쌀 2컵
콩나물 100g
멸치 다시마 국물 2½컵

쇠고기 채소볶음
다진 쇠고기 50g
표고버섯·당근 50g씩
간장 ½큰술
다진 파 2작은술
다진 마늘 1작은술
설탕·참기름·깨소금·식용유 조금씩

달래간장
달래 50g
간장 2큰술
다진 파·마늘 조금씩
고춧가루·설탕 조금씩
참기름·깨소금 조금씩

만드는 법

1 쌀은 불려서 준비하고, 콩나물은 깨끗이 다듬어 놓는다.
2 솥에 불린 쌀과 멸치다시마 국물을 부어 밥을 짓는다. 이때 쌀과 멸치다시마 국물의 비율을 1:1.2로 한다. 밥물이 스며들면 콩나물을 함께 넣고 익힌다.
3 다진 쇠고기는 다진 파·마늘, 간장, 설탕, 참기름, 깨소금을 넣고 양념한다. 표고버섯과 당근은 굵직하게 썬다.
4 팬에 기름을 두르고 양념한 쇠고기를 볶는다. 고기가 익으면 다진 표고버섯과 당근을 넣어 함께 볶는다.
5 달래를 잘게 썰어 나머지 재료와 함께 섞어서 달래간장을 만든다.
6 그릇에 콩나물밥을 담고 ④의 쇠고기 채소볶음을 올려 달래간장으로 비벼 먹는다.

Bean sprouts Bibimbap

This variety is enjoyed with bean sprouts, mushrooms and carrots sautéed and mixed with fragrant soy sauce with wild chive.

Ingredients (2 servings)

Bean sprouts rice
2 cups of soaked rice
100g of bean sprouts
2½ cups of anchovy kelp soup

Fried beef and vegetables
50g of chopped beef
50g of shiitake
50g of carrot
½Ts soy sauce
2ts chopped leek
1ts crushed garlic
a little bit of sesame oil,
sugar, ground sesame
and cooking oil

Wild chive soy sauce
50g of wild chive
2Ts soy sauce
a little bit of chopped leek,
crushed garlic, sugar,
red pepper powder, sesame
oil, and ground sesame

Preparation

1 Soak rice in the water, and prepare bean sprouts.

2 Cook rice with soaked rice and anchovy kelp soup. The ratio of rice and the soup is to be around 1:1.2. When the water is soaked into the rice, boil it with bean sprouts.

3 Chop shiitake and carrots. Season chopped meat with chopped leek, crushed garlic, soy sauce, sugar, sesame oil, and ground sesame.

4 Put oil in a frying pan and sauté seasoned beef. When the beef is done, cook it with chopped shiitakes and carrots.

5 Chop wild chive and mix with other Ingredients to make a dressing.

6 Put bean sprouts rice in a bowl, sautéed beef and vegetables of ④ on and serve it with wild chive sauce.

두부 간장 비빔밥

바삭하게 구운 두부와 향긋한 상추·깻잎을 넣고 간장소스에 비벼 먹는 채식 비빔밥

재료 (2인분)

밥 2공기
두부 1모
소금 2작은술
상추·깻잎·부추 50g씩
후리가케 조금
올리브오일 적당량

초간장

간장 3큰술
설탕 ½큰술
매실액·식초 1큰술씩
고춧가루·깨소금 1작은술씩

만드는 법

1 두부는 작고 네모지게 썰어 소금을 조금 뿌려 둔다.
2 팬에 올리브오일을 두르고 두부를 굽는다.
3 상추와 깻잎은 채 썰고, 부추는 송송 썰어 물에 담가 놓는다.
4 초간장 재료를 한데 넣고 섞는다.
5 그릇에 밥을 담고 채소를 올린 후 구운 두부를 얹는다.
6 두부 위에 후리가케를 뿌리고 초간장을 함께 내 비벼 먹게 한다.

Tofu Bibimbap with Soy sauce

This is a menu for vegetarians, with fried tofu, sweet-smelling lettuce, and sesame leaves on cooked rice and served in soy sauce.

Ingredients (2 servings)

2 bowls of rice
1 tofu
50g of lettuce
50g of sesame leaf
50g of leek
2ts salt
enough olive oil and Hurigake

Soy sauce mixed with vinegar

3Ts soy sauce
½Ts sugar
1Ts plum extract
1Ts vinegar
1ts each of red pepper powder and ground sesame

Preparation

1. Cut tofu into small pieces and in squire shape, and add a dash of salt.
2. Cook tofu in a frying pan.
3. Shred lettuce, sesame leaves and leeks and soak them in water.
4. Mix the ingredient for soy sauce and mix it with vinegar.
5. Put cooked rice in a bowl. Place vegetables and tofu on the bed of rice.
6. Put Hurigake on tofu and serve it with the soy sauce mixed with vinegar.

도토리묵 비빔밥

도토리묵과 배추김치를 이용해 만든 비빔밥. 묵은 칼로리가 거의 없는 대표적인 다이어트 식품이다.

재료 (2인분)

밥 2공기
파프리카·오이 ½개씩
상추·깻잎·쑥갓 50g씩

도토리묵 무침

도토리묵 ¼모
참기름 ½큰술
소금 조금

김치 무침

김치 100g
참기름·설탕·통깨 ½큰술씩

양념간장

다진 파 3큰술
간장 3큰술
고춧가루·깨소금·
설탕·참기름 조금씩

만드는 법

1 도토리묵은 4cm 길이로 굵게 채 썰어 참기름과 소금으로 버무린다.
2 김치는 잘게 썰어 물기를 꼭 짠 후 참기름, 설탕, 통깨를 넣고 무친다.
3 파프리카는 반 갈라 채 썰고, 오이는 4cm 길이로 토막내 돌려 깎아 가늘게 채 썬다.
4 상추, 깻잎, 쑥갓은 묵과 비슷한 길이로 가늘게 채 썬다.
5 그릇에 따뜻한 밥을 담고 채 썬 채소와 도토리묵, 양념한 김치를 올린다.
6 양념간장을 만들어 ⑤의 묵밥에 넣고 비벼 먹는다.

Acorn jello Bibimbap

Because of its low calories, acorn jello is a representative diet food. This is a kind of jello bibimbap with acorn jello and kimchi.

Ingredients (2 servings)

2 bowls of rice
½ cucumber
½ paprika
50g of lettuce
50g of sesame leaf
50g of crown daisy

Seasoned acorn jello
¼ acorn jello
½Ts sesame oil
a little salt

Seasoned kimchi
100g of kimchi
½Ts sesame oil, sugar, sesame

Seasoned soy sauce
3Ts chopped leek
3Ts of soy sauce
a little bit of sesame oil,
sugar, red pepper powder,
and ground sesame

Preparation

1. Chop acorn jello in 4cm length and season it with sesame oil and salt.
2. Chopping Kimchi and get rid of water. Season it with sugar, sesame and sesame oil.
3. Chop paprika in 4cm length and chop the skin of cucumber as in 4cm.
4. Chop lettuce, sesame leaf, and crown daisy in the same length with acorn jello.
5. Put warm cooked rice in a bowl and put chopped vegetables, acorn jello and seasoned kimchi on it.
6. Make seasoned soy sauce and put it in the acorn jello rice of ⑤ and serve it.

비빔 쌈밥

익힌 채소로 쌈을 싸 소화도 잘 되고 건강에도 좋은 쌈밥. 다시마나 미역을 사용해도 좋다.

재료 (2인분)

기본 비빔밥
밥 2공기
나물 또는 채소 적당량
고추장 3큰술
물엿 ½큰술
참기름 조금

호박잎 6장
양배추 잎 6장
적양배추 잎 6장

골뱅이쌈장
골뱅이 2큰술
쌈장 3큰술
다진 파 ½큰술
다진 마늘 2작은술
다진 고추 2작은술
물엿 ½큰술
깨소금 1작은술

만드는 법

1 따뜻한 밥에 채소, 나물 등 있는 재료를 다져 넣고 고추장, 물엿, 참기름으로 비벼서 기본 비빔밥을 만든다.

2 호박잎은 찜통에 살짝 찐다.

3 양배추와 적양배추는 굵은 심을 잘라내고 소금물에 살짝 데친다.

4 골뱅이를 잘게 다진 후 나머지 재료와 섞어서 골뱅이쌈장을 만든다.

5 호박잎, 양배추 잎, 적양배추 잎을 한 장씩 펼쳐 놓고 ①의 비빔밥을 한 숟가락 올린 뒤 골뱅이 쌈장을 조금 넣어 돌돌 만다.

Bibimbap with Vegetable wraps

This Bibimbap is made of cooked vegetables that are easy to digest and healthy. You can use kelp or seaweed.

Ingredients (2 servings)

Basic bibimbap
2 bowls of cooked rice
enough Namul or herbs
3Ts red pepper paste
½Ts starch syrup
a little sesame oil

6 leaves of pumpkin leaf
6 leaves of cabbage
6 leaves of red cabbage

Whelk ssam-jang
2Ts whelk
3Ts ssam-jang
½Ts chopped leek
2ts crushed garlic
2ts chopped pepper
½Ts starch syrup
1ts ground sesame

Preparation

1. Make basic bibimbap by putting chopped Namul(seasoned vegetable) or herbs in warm rice and mixing it with red pepper paste, starch syrup and sesame oil.
2. Steam pumpkin leaves slightly.
3. Cut out the cores of cabbage and red cabbage and parboil them slightly in salt water.
4. Make whelk ssam-jang by mincing whelk into small pieces and mixing it with other Ingredients.
5. Spread one piece of each pumpkin leaf, cabbage, red cabbage, put 1 spoon of Bibimbap from ① add whelk ssam-jang and roll.

무생채 비빔밥

매콤 새콤하게 양념한 무생채를 두반장 소스로 비벼 특별한 맛이 나는 간단 비빔밥

재료 (2인분)

밥 2공기

무생채
무 200g
양파 ½개
대파 ½대
고운 고춧가루 1큰술
다진 파·생강즙 1작은술씩
다진 마늘 ½큰술
멸치액젓·설탕·식초 ½큰술씩
깨소금·소금 조금씩

두반장 고추 소스
두반장 ½컵
배즙 2큰술
다진 고추 1큰술
송송 썬 실파 1큰술
꿀 ½큰술
참기름 1작은술
소금 조금

만드는 법

1. 무는 껍질을 벗기고 곱게 채 썬다.
2. 양파와 대파는 가늘게 채 썰어 찬물에 담가 매운맛을 뺀 뒤 건져서 물기를 뺀다.
3. 채 썬 무에 고춧가루를 버무려 물을 들인 후 설탕, 식초, 소금에 잠시 절인다.
4. 무가 적당히 절여져서 숨이 죽으면 물기를 짠 후 채 썬 양파와 대파, 다진 파, 다진 마늘, 생강즙, 멸치액젓, 깨소금을 넣고 함께 무친다.
5. 재료를 모두 섞어 두반장 고추 소스를 만든다. 송송 썬 실파는 맨 나중에 섞는다.
6. 그릇에 따뜻한 밥을 담고 무생채를 올린 후 두반장 고추 소스를 끼얹는다.

> **Tip** 채 썬 무를 미리 고춧가루에 버무린 다음에 다른 양념을 넣어 무치는 것이 포인트. 고춧가루를 다른 양념과 함께 넣고 무치면 고춧가루가 겉돌아 색이 예쁘지 않다.

1

2

5

Spicy Radish Salad Bibimbap

Simple Bibimbap with Spicy Radish Salad and Doubanjiang sauce.

Ingredients (2 servings)

2 bowls of cooked rice

Spicy Radish Salad
200g of radish
½ each of onion and leek
1ts chopped leek
½Ts crushed garlic
1ts ginger juice
1Ts red pepper powder
½Ts salted anchovy sauce
½Ts sugar
½Ts vinegar
a little salt and ground sesame

Doubanjiang Green pepper sauce
½ cup of doubanjiang
2Ts pear juice
1Ts chopped green pepper
1Ts sliced leek
½Ts honey
1ts sesame oil
a little salt

Preparation

1 Peel and shred the radish.

2 Slice the onion and leek, then soak them in cold water to remove spicy and squeeze out water.

3 Mix and red pepper powder to color, then add the sugar, vinegar and salt and wait for a while.

4 When radishes are properly pickled squeeze the water out, then add chopped onions·leek, crushed garlic, ginger juice, anchovy sauce, ground sesame and season them together.

5 Make Doubanjiang Green pepper sauce to mix the seasoning ingredients, then put sliced leeks.

6 Prepare cooked rice and spicy radish salad and mix it with Doubanjiang Green pepper sauce in a bowl.

Tip The key point is to mix shredded radish with the red pepper powder first.

Chapter

Traditional Bibimbap 전통 비빔밥

Traditional bibimbap which has unique flavor with regional ingredient. Bibimbaps such as the national recipe, Jeonju-style bibimbap, Andong-style Bibimbap which originated from ritual food and Tongyoung-style bibimbap with seaweed have a distinct characteristic.

각 지역의 특산물이 들어가 독특한 맛을 자랑하는 향토 비빔밥. 비빔밥의 대표격인 전주 비빔밥, 제사 음식에서 유래가 된 안동 비빔밥, 해초가 들어간 통영 비빔밥 등은 지역의 특색을 잘 나타낸다.

전주 비빔밥

여러 가지 나물과 육회를 밥 위에 올리고 고추장에 비벼먹는 우리나라 대표 비빔밥

재료 (2인분)

밥 2공기
은행·잣 조금씩
달걀 2개

쇠고기 육회
쇠고기 50g
다진 파·마늘 조금씩
배즙·청주·간장·참기름·깨소금·
잣가루·후춧가루 조금씩

각종 나물 (40g씩)
콩나물·애호박나물·
도라지나물·고사리나물·
무나물·미나리나물
당근볶음·표고버섯볶음

달걀지단
달걀 2개
소금·식용유 조금씩

양념고추장
고추장 3큰술, 물엿 1큰술,
매실액 ½큰술,
다진 마늘·참기름 조금씩

만드는 법

1 물에 불린 쌀로 밥을 지어 밥 2공기를 준비한다.
2 쇠고기는 채 썰어 다진 파, 다진 마늘, 배즙, 청주, 간장, 잣가루, 후춧가루, 참기름, 깨소금을 넣고 양념해서 육회로 준비한다.
3 콩나물·애호박나물·도라지나물·고사리나물·미나리나물·무나물을 조금씩 준비한다. 당근볶음과 표고버섯볶음도 준비한다. (p.18-21 참조)
4 달걀은 노른자만 분리해 2개는 지단을 부쳐서 채 썰고, 2개는 따로 준비한다.
5 그릇에 따뜻한 밥을 담고 준비한 나물과 달걀지단 채를 돌려 담는다. 나물 가운데 쇠고기 육회와 달걀노른자를 올리고 은행과 잣가루로 장식한다.
6 양념고추장을 만들어 비벼 먹는다.

 **Tip** 기호에 따라 참기름에 무친 청포묵을 넣는다.

1

2

3

Jeonju-style Bibimbap

This well-known bibimbap is a bowl of rice topped with Namul and Beef yukhoe, which is to be later mixed with Gochujang.

Ingredients (2 servings)

2 bowls of cooked rice
a little ginko nut and pine nut
2 eggs

Beef yukhoe
50g of beef
a little bit of pear juice,
chopped leek, crushed garlic,
soy sauce, ground sesame,
rice wine, ground pepper,
and ground pine nuts

Seasoned vegetables (40g each)
bean sprouts, zucchini, bellflower root, bracken, radish and water parsley, shiitake, carrot

Egg Jidan
2 eggs
a little bit of cooking oil

Seasoned red pepper paste
3Ts red pepper paste
1Ts starch syrup
½Ts plum extract
a little bit of crushed garlic, sesame oil

Preparation

1. Soak some rice in water and then, cook two servings of the rice.
2. Thinly slice the meat. Next, season it with pear juice, rice wine, chopped leek, crushed garlic, soy sauce, ground pine nuts, ground pepper, sesame oil and roasted sesame seeds.
3. Prepare each of the seasoned bean sprouts, zucchini, bellflower root, bracken, raw radish and water parsley. Shred carrots and shiitake, then sauté them with a dash of salt. (see p.22-25)
4. Beat the eggs and spread them on a frying pan. Once cooked, thinly slice them.
5. Place cooked rice in a bowl and arrange vegetables and sliced egg in circle. Beef yukhoe and egg yolk can be placed in the middle and decorate it with ginko nuts and ground pine nuts.
6. Serve everything stirred together with seasoned red pepper paste.

> **Tip** You can also add Cheongpomuk(mung bean jelly) seasoned with sesame oil.

1

2

3

평양 비빔밥

북한의 대표 비빔밥. 채 썬 쇠고기볶음과 숙주나물이 들어가는 게 특징이다.

재료 (2인분)

밥 2공기
김 1장

쇠고기 볶음
쇠고기 50g
다진 파 1작은술
다진 마늘 ½작은술
간장·설탕·깨소금·참기름 1작은술씩
후춧가루·식용유 조금씩

각종 나물 (40g씩)
숙주나물·시금치나물·
도라지나물·고사리나물·당근볶음

달걀지단
달걀 2개
소금·식용유 조금씩

양념고추장
고추장 3큰술
물엿 1큰술
매실액 ½큰술
다진 마늘 2작은술
참기름 2작은술

만드는 법

1. 물에 불린 쌀로 밥을 지어 밥 2공기를 준비한다.
2. 쇠고기는 채 썬 뒤 다진 파, 다진 마늘, 간장, 설탕, 깨소금, 참기름, 후춧가루로 양념해서 볶는다.
3. 숙주나물·시금치나물·도라지나물·고사리나물·당근볶음을 준비한다. (p.18-21 참조)
4. 달걀은 흰자와 노른자를 나눠서 얇게 황백 지단을 부쳐서 채 썰고, 일부는 마름모 꼴로 썬다.
5. 김을 구워서 손으로 잘게 부순다.
6. 그릇에 따뜻한 밥을 담고 나물과 채 썬 달걀지단, 김가루를 올린 다음, 가운데 볶은 쇠고기를 올리고 달걀지단으로 장식한다.
7. 양념고추장을 만들어 비벼 먹는다.

Pyongyang-style Bibimbap

A signature bibimbap of North Korea.
It is characterized by fried beef and seasoned green bean sprouts.

Ingredients (2 servings)

2 bowls of cooked rice
1 sheet of dried seaweed

Fried beef
50g of beef
1ts chopped leek
½ts crushed garlic
1ts each of soy sauce, sugar, ground sesame, sesame oil
a little bit of ground pepper and cooking oil

Seasoned vegetables (40g each)
bean sprouts, spinach, bracken, bellflower roots, fried carrot

Egg Jidan
2 eggs
a little bit of salt, cooking oil

Seasoned red pepper paste
3Ts red pepper paste
1Ts starch syrup
½Ts plum extract
2ts crushed garlic
2ts sesame oil

Preparation

1. Soak some rice in water. Then prepare two bowls of cooked rice.
2. After thinly slicing the beef, sauté it with chopped leek, crushed garlic, soy sauce, sugar, roasted sesame seeds, sesame oil and ground pepper.
3. Prepare each of the seasoned bean sprouts, spinach, bellflower roots, bracken and fried carrot. (see p.22-25)
4. Separate the egg yolk from the white and each cook on a frying pan thinly. Then, slice some of them and cut the rest into diamond.
5. Lightly toast a sheet of dried seaweed and crush it with your hand into pieces.
6. Place cooked rice in a bowl, seasoned vegetables, sliced egg jidan and crushed dried seaweed. In the middle, put fried beef and garnish with egg jidan.
7. Serve everything stirred together with seasoned red pepper paste.

안동 비빔밥

제사를 지내고 남은 나물과 전 등을 한데 넣고 비벼 먹는 비빔밥. 양념간장으로 비벼 담백하다.

재료 (2인분)

밥 2공기
식용유 조금

쇠고기 산적
쇠고기 50g
다진 파 1작은술
다진 마늘 ½작은술
간장·청주·설탕·후춧가루 조금씩

전
동태살 저민 것 2장
두부 저민 것 2장
소금·후춧가루 조금씩
밀가루 2큰술
달걀 푼 것 1개분

각종 나물 (40g씩)
콩나물·시금치나물·무나물·배추볶음
나물·고사리나물·도라지나물

양념간장
간장 3큰술
다진 파 2작은술
다진 마늘·참기름 1작은술씩
통깨 조금

만드는 법

1 쇠고기는 다진 파, 다진 마늘, 간장, 설탕, 청주, 후춧가루로 양념한다.
2 쇠고기에 양념이 배면 기름 두른 팬에 굽는다.
3 동태와 두부는 소금, 후춧가루로 양념한 다음 밀가루를 묻히고 달걀 푼 물에 담갔다가 기름 두른 팬에 지진다.
4 콩나물·시금치나물·무나물·배추볶음나물·고사리나물·도라지나물을 조금씩 준비한다. (p.18-21 참조)
5 그릇에 따뜻한 밥을 담고 준비한 나물과 동태전, 두부전, 쇠고기 산적을 올린다.
6 양념간장 재료를 섞어서 비빔밥과 함께 상에 낸다.

3

4

4

Andong-style Bibimbap

Clean taste of bibimbap, served with left over seasoned vegetables and jeon(Korean pancakes) from ancestral rites.

Ingredients (2 servings)

2 bowls of cooked rice
a little cooking oil

Beef sanjeok
50g of beef
1ts chopped leek
½ts crushed garlic
a little ground pepper

Jeon
2 slices of frozen pollack
2 slices of cooked tofu
a little salt and pepper
2Ts flour, 1 whipped egg

Seasoned vegetables (40g each)
bean sprouts, spinach,
bracken, bellflower root,
radish, kimchi cabbage

Seasoned soy sauce
3Ts soy sauce
2ts chopped leek
1ts crushed garlic
1ts sesame oil
a little sesame

Preparation

1. Season the meat with chopped leek, crushed garlic, soy sauce, sugar, rice wine and ground pepper.

2. After the meat is seasoned, sauté it on a frying pan with some cooking oil.

3. Season the frozen pollack and tofu with ground pepper. Then coat them with flour and place the pollack in whipped egg. Put the coated pollack on a frying pan.

4. Prepare each of the seasoned bean sprouts, spinach, radish, kimchi cabbage, bracken and bellflower roots. (see p.22-25)

5. Place prepared vegetables, sanjeok and fried tofu on a bed of warm rice.

6. Mix the ingredients with seasoned soy sauce and serve with bibimbap.

3

4

4

통영 비빔밥

톳, 청각 등의 해초와 나물을 이용한 건강식. 조선 시대부터 내려오는 전통 비빔밥이다.

재료 (2인분)

불린 쌀 2컵
홍합·바지락 50g씩
참기름 1작은술
물 2컵
청각·톳 40g씩
은행·잣 조금씩

쇠고기 육회

쇠고기 50g
다진 파·마늘 조금씩
배즙·청주·간장·깨소금·참기름·
잣가루·후춧가루 조금씩

각종 나물 (40g씩)

콩나물·숙주나물·시금치나물·
애호박나물·가지나물·도라지나물·
고사리나물

달걀지단

달걀노른자 1개
소금·식용유 조금씩

양념고추장

고추장 3큰술, 물엿 1큰술
매실액 ½큰술
다진 마늘·참기름 2작은술씩

만드는 법

1 홍합과 바지락 살을 곱게 다져서 냄비에 넣고 참기름을 조금 두르고 볶는다. 여기에 불린 쌀을 넣고 물을 부어서 밥을 짓는다.
2 쇠고기는 채 썰어 배즙, 청주, 다진 파, 다진 마늘, 간장, 잣가루, 후춧가루, 참기름, 깨소금으로 양념한다.
3 콩나물·숙주나물·시금치나물·애호박나물·가지나물·도라지나물·고사리나물을 조금씩 준비한다. (p.18~21 참조)
4 청각과 톳은 깨끗이 씻어 물기를 꼭 짠다.
5 달걀노른자를 풀어서 팬에 얇게 부친 후 채 썬다.
6 그릇에 밥을 담고 준비한 나물과 해초를 담는다. 가운데 육회를 올리고 은행, 잣으로 장식한 다음 양념고추장을 만들어 비벼 먹는다.

Tip 기호에 따라 참기름에 무친 청포묵을 넣는다.

1

2

3

4

Tongyoung-style Bibimbap

A healthy dish made with seaweed such as sponge seaweed, fusiformis, and herbs. This is a traditional bibimbap from the Joseon Dynasty.

Ingredients (2 servings)

2 cups of rice soaked in water
50g each of mussel, manila clam
1ts sesame oil
2 cups of water, 40g each of sponge seaweed, fusiformis
a little ginkgo nut and pine nut

Beef yukhoe
50g of beef
a little bit of rice wine, pear juice, chopped leek, crushed garlic, soy sauce, sesame oil, ground sesame, ground pine nuts, pepper

Seasoned vegetables (40g each)
bean sprouts, green bean sprouts, spinach, zucchini, eggplant, bellflower roots, bracken

Egg Jidan
1 egg yolk
a little bit of cooking oil

Seasoned red pepper paste
3Ts red pepper paste
1Ts starch syrup
½ts plum extract
2ts crushed garlic, sesame oil

Preparation

1. Finely chop the fleshy part of mussels and manila clams. Then sauté them with a little of sesame oil in a pot. Put soaked rice in and cook the rice.

2. Shred the meat and sauté with pear juice, rice wine, chopped leek, crushed garlic, soy sauce, ground pine nuts, pepper, sesame oil and ground sesame.

3. Prepare each of the seasoned bean sprouts, green bean sprouts, spinach, zucchini, eggplants, bellflower roots and bracken. (see p.22-25)

4. Rinse sponge seaweed and fusiformis. Make sure to squeeze them dry.

5. Beat the egg and spread it on a frying pan. When cooked, slice it thinly.

6. Place the rice with prepared vegetables and seaweeds. In the middle, place raw meat slices and decorate the dish with ginko nuts and pine nuts. Stir together with seasoned red pepper paste.

Tip You can also add Cheongpomuk(mung bean jelly) seasoned with sesame oil.

평안도 비빔밥

삶은 닭고기를 고춧가루 양념으로 무치고 콩나물, 애호박나물과 함께 비벼 먹는 여름철 별미 요리

재료 (2인분)

밥 2공기

닭고기 무침

닭 ½마리
대파 1뿌리
마늘 3쪽
생강 1톨
고춧가루 1큰술
다진 마늘 ½큰술
간장·꿀 2작은술씩
깨소금 1작은술

각종 나물 (80g씩)

콩나물·애호박나물

양념고추장

고추장 3큰술
물엿 1큰술
매실액 ½큰술
다진 마늘·참기름 2작은술씩

만드는 법

1 냄비에 물을 넉넉히 붓고 닭과 대파, 마늘, 생강을 넣어 1시간 정도 푹 삶는다.
2 삶은 닭고기는 살만 떼어서 가늘게 찢은 다음 다진 마늘, 고춧가루, 간장, 꿀, 깨소금을 넣어 무친다.
3 콩나물과 애호박나물을 조금씩 준비한다. (p.18-21 참조)
4 양념고추장 재료를 한데 섞는다.
5 그릇에 밥을 담고 양념한 닭고기와 콩나물, 애호박나물을 함께 담는다.
6 그 위에 양념고추장을 올려서 비벼 먹는다.

1

2

3

Pyongahndo-style Bibimbap

This bibimbap mixes bean sprouts and zucchini with chicken, after it is boiled and marinated. It is a special delicacy for summer.

Ingredients (2 servings)

2 bowls of cooked rice

Seasoned chicken
½ chicken
1 leek
3 pieces of garlic
1 piece of ginger
1Ts red pepper powder
½ts crushed garlic
2ts soy sauce
2ts honey
1ts ground sesame

Seasoned vegetables (80g each)
been sprouts
zucchini

Seasoned red pepper paste
3Ts red pepper paste
1Ts starch syrup
½Ts plum extract
2ts crushed garlic
2ts sesame oil

Preparation

1. Boil the chicken with leek, garlic, ginger, and plenty of water in a pot for about an hour.
2. Tear the boiled chicken into thin pieces and season it with red pepper powder, crushed garlic, soy sauce, honey, ground sesame.
3. Prepare bean sprouts and zucchini. (see p.22-25)
4. Mix the seasoning ingredients to make seasoning red pepper paste.
5. Put the warm cooked rice in the bowl and place seasoned chicken, bean sprouts, and zucchini together.
6. Mix it with seasoned red pepper paste and serve.

Glossary of Korean Cooking

Food & Ingredients

Kimchi cabbage The main ingredient of Kimchi. Season after parboiling or roasting. When making Kimchi, ferment it after preserving it in salt.

Radish Koreans enjoy eating white radish. Season either after cutting it raw or stir-fry it. You can use it as an ingredient for pickles or Kkakdugi.

Yeolmu Young radish. You can either make Kimchi or parboil and marinate. The dried version is called 'Siraegi'.

Bean sprouts Grown by budding soybean sprouts. Season after parboiling it.

Green bean sprouts Grown by budding mungbean sprouts. Season after parboiling it like bean sprouts.

Spinach Unlike in the Western culture where spinach is eaten raw, in Korea you eat it after parboiling and lightly seasoned.

Doraji Bellflower roots. It has a bitter taste but you eat it seasoned after fermenting it in salt or sautéing it.

Gosa-ri Bracken. After drying the tender stem, parboil and fry then season.

Chi-namul Aster. Unique fragrant wild vegetable. Like Gosa-ri, dry it before parboiling and seasoning.

Minari Water parsley. Season it raw or after frying it.

Kkaennip The leaves of sesame. Parboil, fry then season. It has a nice fragrance so it's good with meat cuisine.

Buchu Chive. It's a herb that is longer and stronger in fragrance than leek. It can be used raw with seasoning or as an ingredient to Kimchi.

Dal-lae Wild chive. It's a herb that is slimmer than leeks. It can be used in salads or within seasoning when sliced in small pieces.

Leek There are two different types: shallot and scallion. Cut into small pieces and use it in seasonings.

Shiitake You can eat it right after collecting or after drying and soaking it in water.

Dried seaweed It's sold in paper-like dried form. You can use it as food decoration after roasting it.

Gochu-jang Red pepper paste. Using red pepper powder as the main ingredient, its thick and spicy flavor is made by fermenting.

Gan-jang Soy sauce. A salty black sauce made by fermented beans.

Doen-jang Soybean paste. A brown thick sauce made by fermented beans.

Ssam-jang A sauce made by mixing together Gochu-jang, Doen-jang and other seasonings.

Cham-gireum An oil made by squeezing the sesame seeds. It's used in almost all seasoned vegetables to extract flavor.

Ground sesame A condiment made by crushing the sesame seeds. It's used in almost all seasoned vegetables for fragrance.

Red pepper powder A powder made by drying red pepper. It's used to add spicy flavor.

Rice wine A liquor made by filtering out the clear water in fermented rice. It's used to get rid of the smell of meat and fish.

Plum extract A concentrate made by fermenting green plum in sugar.

Salted anchovy sauce A sauce made by fermented anchovy.

Anchovy soup A soup made by brewing Anchovy in hot water.

Kelp soup A soup made by brewing kelp in hot water.

Kimchi Korean pickle that is made by fermenting salted kimchi cabbage seasoned with red pepper powder, leek and garlic.

Beef yukhoe Sliced fresh raw beef with various seasonings.

Bulgogi A dish in which beef is cooked after being marinated.

Dduk-galbi Shaping the minced rib meat after seasoning.

Dotori-muk A jelly-like dish made of acorn powder.

Cheongpomuk A jelly-like dish made of mung bean powder.

Starch syrup A syrup made by starch such as rice, corn, millet and sweet potato, etc.

Egg Jidan A type of garnish made from thinly cooked eggs.

Jeon Korean-style pancake made with flour and egg covering fish, vegetables and meat.

Sanjuk A dish made with fish, vegetables, mushrooms and meat on a stick.

Cooking Techniques

Stir Mixing ingredients together.

Sauté Cook food on a frying pan with a little bit of oil.

Season Mix vegetables with condiments.

Parboil Slightly boil food in boiling water.

Shred Thinly slice ingredients like vegetables.

All The Rice Dishes in The World 뚝딱! 한 그릇 밥

This book contains 76 kinds of rice in the world such as topped rice, fried rice, bibimbap. It's a one meal cooking book that has various menus from Korean food to exotic food of other countries. It's better because you can easily make it with the ingredients in the refrigerator.

216 pages | 188×245mm | April 2021 | ₩14,000 | ISBN 9791156162100

All The Noodles in The World 뚝딱! 한 그릇 국수

If you want a light and delicious meal, noodles are perfect. This book introduces 63 noodle recipes, including bibim noodles, noodle soup, stir fried noodles etc. This book also provides information on basic techniques for making noodle dishes, how to make noodle soup.

200 pages | 188×245mm | July 2021 | ₩14,000 | ISBN 9791156162261

I Love Salad 샐러드에 반하다

This book introduces a simple and delicious salad. It consists of salads that can be easily made from readily available materials around it. The book shows the calories of the dressing and the total calories separately, so you can control the calories yourself.

184 pages | 210×256mm | May 2021 | ₩16,000 | ISBN 9791156162124

Every Snacks 술에는 안주

This book introduces 64 types of snacks that best bring out the taste of alcohol and the atmosphere of a drinking party by category. Each recipe is meticulously packed with friendly tips, so everyone can make delicious snacks. All information about alcohol is included in this book.

152 pages | 151×205mm | December 2022 | ₩13,000 | ISBN 9791156162926

Cocktail at Home 칵테일 앳 홈

The book is an original and reproduced version of the cocktail recipe that was popular among YouTube subscribers. There are 85 recipes, ranging from familiar cocktails to unique cocktails. It is categorized by type of alcohol, and the alcoholicity is also indicated.

208 pages | 146×205mm | January 2024 | ₩18,000 | ISBN 9791156163206